SILENT CITIES:
NEW YORK

HIDDEN HISTORIES OF THE
REGION'S CEMETERIES

JESSICA FERRI

Globe
Pequot

Guilford, Connecticut

For Graham, my favorite New Yorker

Globe Pequot

An imprint of The Rowman & Littlefield Publishing Group, Inc.
4501 Forbes Blvd., Ste. 200
Lanham, MD 20706
www.rowman.com

Distributed by NATIONAL BOOK NETWORK

British Library Cataloguing in Publication Information available

Library of Congress Control Number 2020932247

ISBN 978-1-4930-4734-5 (paper : alk. paper)
ISBN 978-1-4930-4735-2 (electronic)

♾™ The paper used in this publication meets the minimum requirements of American National Standard for Information Sciences—Permanence of Paper for Printed Library Materials, ANSI/NISO Z39.48-1992.

TABLE OF CONTENTS

"Being dead, yet speaketh . . ."

HEBREWS 11:4

INTRODUCTION

I WAS HERE

I moved to New York just twelve days after my twenty-first birthday. I had never set foot in Brooklyn. My mom and I got off the plane and into a cab at LaGuardia airport.

"We're going to Bushwick," my mom told the driver, and she gave him the address.

"Okay," he said. "Why?"

Thirteen years later, I'm married, I have a two-year-old son, and I'm leaving New York.

But New York casts a long shadow.

Every single time I came home to New York, I got in a cab and made the drive home to Brooklyn via the Brooklyn Queens Expressway. Every single time I left home in Brooklyn to drive to the airport, I made the same journey in the opposite direction.

Outside my window was a massive mirror image of Manhattan: thousands upon thousands of small standing stones that make up Calvary Cemetery, the largest cemetery in the United States of America.

New York is the city that never sleeps. But there is an entire separate city, a twin, that does. The cemeteries of New York are cities in their own right. Silent cities.

Calvary Cemetery was there to welcome me to Brooklyn. It was still there, thirteen years later, when I flew out of New York as a New Yorker for the last time.

I always wanted to live in New York. I think it was an early passion for music and theater that gave me the idea. I wanted to sing under the bright lights of Broadway. In reality, my own journey to becoming a New Yorker was more circuitous than the plot of *Fame*. But I spent the most formative years of my life in New York, so it will always feel like home to me.

A city like New York subsists off the energy that is infused into it every day. As the capital of commerce and culture, New York is an adopted home, a spiritual home, for many Americans.

Time passes here at an alarming rate. The pace of the city is not for everyone. But the clip at which the city changes makes it the best city it can be. There's no time for anyone or anything to resist that change. As many tombstones remind us, "Tempus fugit." Time flies.

Americans have a complex relationship with our history. We are a young country, and the truth of our history is still being revealed. For hundreds of years, what went into the canon and what was preserved was chosen by a select few with select interests.

New York expands, warps, and pops back into shape at every moment. This kind of rapid development is not what we usually associate with cemeteries, which are, quite literally, set in stone.

These silent cities speak volumes. They persevere, standing still amidst the humming volume of the living city.

Outside of Calvary Cemetery looking in, its size is what strikes you. Inside Calvary, it's the same feeling but on the micro level. Every single stone tells a story of immigrants, of generation upon generation of people who came here to become Americans via New York.

Just a short drive into Queens is Mount Zion Cemetery, one of the largest Jewish cemeteries in the United States. The stones are stacked nearly on top of each other, like sardines. A walk through reveals hundreds of thousands of gravestones, undulating like the gigantic gray sea. There are so many people. The cemetery was busiest from the 1930s to the 1950s. These Jewish people died here, in their adopted home. By doing so, they survived.

I was walking back to the subway after a doctor's appointment in the West Village one afternoon when something caught my eye: a few rounded pebbles placed on a gate. I turned to look more closely and realized there was a small cemetery wedged between two buildings. The gravestones, long weathered, were propped up against the brick wall of the alley. This is the second cemetery of the congregation of Shearith Israel, the oldest Jewish congregation in America and one of the oldest Jewish cemeteries in the country.

And it's just wedged here on West Eleventh Street, like a misplaced library book.

Construction of a federal office building in Lower Manhattan in 1991 revealed the African Burial Ground, a sacred graveyard of the enslaved, the resting place of upwards of fifteen thousand people.

In Orient Beach State Park, at the tippy-top of Long Island, there is a small "slaves burying ground." A bright blue plaque explains that this is also the resting place of the slave owners, Seth and Maria Tuthill: "It was their wish that they be buried with their former servants."

Their former servants.

There was a howling wet wind the day I made my way to this small graveyard, with a broken umbrella, wishing I'd worn another layer of clothing. The Tuthills' graves are marked with stones bearing their names and dates. Their slaves' graves are marked by shells.

Like most writers, I'm obsessed with stories and the ways in which people tell their stories. A tombstone is an abbreviated record of a life lived, like an entry in a search engine. Sometimes there's not much more than a name and two dates separated by that small dash. "Live your dash," people say.

In the same way that a gravestone is a record of a person's life, cemeteries are the stories of a place. Gigantic cemeteries like Calvary and Mount Zion speak to the history of immigration in New York and this country as a whole. Park cemeteries like Brooklyn's Green-Wood tell the story of urban development and the modern American metropolis. And each reflects American's changing attitudes toward death and dying. Even an incredibly small cemetery, like the burying ground in Orient, set back from the dirt road and protected by a small rickety white gate, tells us an enormous lot about our history.

We are surrounded by our past, but so often, these silent cities are pushed to the wayside, isolated, neglected, and ultimately forgotten. The important stories of a people and a place, by proxy, are lost.

People are pretty weirded out when I tell them about *Silent Cities*. Frankly I get a kick out of breezing into a bar and telling people I've spent the morning in a cemetery. "That's a little *morbid*," they laugh. "You're a regular Wednesday Addams."

But until the Civil War, to take a stroll in a cemetery was a very normal activity for most Americans who were committed to the idea of the Good Death, the belief that under certain circumstances, death could be a positive thing.

Today we call the Good Death the Death Positive, or Death Pos, movement. Like Sex Positivity, proponents of the Death Positive philosophy want to encourage people to speak openly about death and dying and have a plan in place for their own deaths. It's the hope that an honest discussion and acknowledgment that life ends will help people to lead better lives.

The revitalization of cemeteries as places to frequent and nourish and protect goes hand in hand with the tenets of Death Positivity. With the rise of cremation, and the medicalization of death (the fact that most people die in hospitals rather than at home), death has been pushed to the outskirts of our consciousness. When death does occur, in our modern society, people can feel at a loss on how to comfort a grieving friend or how to grieve themselves. Death doesn't quite feel real, until, of course, it is undeniably so.

The next time I fly into New York, it won't be to come home.

I'll be visiting. A visitor.

In a sense, we're all just visiting. New York was my home for over a decade, but exploring cemeteries and unlocking their secrets made me feel like a tourist in my adopted home. I think this is a good thing. A sense of curiosity even our daily routines can be life-changing.

When I was young, my family would make the roughly eight-hour drive from our home north of Atlanta down to Florida to visit my grandfather. Aside from the unavoidable bathroom breaks and fast food drive-throughs, we would stop in the small town in south Georgia where my grandfather and grandmother grew up. It's the kind of place that you'd drive right past on a road trip. There's only one traffic light and not much else except farmland—in fact, my family farmed cotton there before, during, and after the Civil War. Off a dusty road of Georgia red clay, there's a small white church with an adjoining cemetery, the resting place of generations upon generations of my mother's family—including the grave of her mother.

I never had a chance to meet my grandma. She died before I was born, when my mother was in her twenties. Even as a child I knew that this great loss was not the kind you forget. I wasn't quite sure what to say to my mother to comfort her. And when we'd stop on the way to Papa's to visit her grave, my mother would stand, the hot sun bearing down on her tanned arms, and say simply, "Here she is." These trips to the cemetery always felt rushed. We all could sense it was difficult for my mom to be there. Now, as an adult, I wonder about what she was thinking, or how I could have comforted her. It always felt like we had to get back on the road, to make it to my grandpa's house before dark. As a curious child I always wanted to stay longer.

One trip I took a handful of gravel from the grave and put it in a pill bottle. I held on to it for years. When we arrived at Papa's house, I remember overhearing my mother say to him, almost in passing, "We stopped to see Mama." If he had any response, I can't recall it.

One visit I must have been in the eighth or ninth grade because I was going through a phase where I wore about ten thousand jelly bracelets and cheap metal bangles on both arms. As we turned to go back to the car I slid one of the bangles off my right arm. It was purple and sparkled in the sun. I placed it on top of my grandma's tombstone and jogged back to the car parked on the dirt road.

When we returned the following year, I wondered if the bracelet would still be there. It wasn't. My mother said something about the church doing a good job keeping up the grounds and that they had probably discarded it. But did they know, I wondered, that it was gift, from a granddaughter to a grandma she had never known, as if to say, "I was here."

A WALK IN THE PARK

GREEN-WOOD CEMETERY, BROOKLYN

On a sunny summer morning, I rounded a corner path at Green-Wood Cemetery, on my way to see one of my favorite monuments. It was very early; the gates had just opened. I wanted to get out there because it was already ninety-three degrees, and I was seven months pregnant.

The monument belongs to a girl named Charlotte Canda who was killed in a carriage accident coming home from her seventeenth birthday party in Manhattan in 1845. At this time of year Green-Wood lives up to its name: it was verdant throughout the cemetery, but particularly vibrant on the patch of land that belongs to Charlotte. Her ornate, Gothic-style memorial, recently cleaned, gleamed ghostly white against the bright green grass.

I have seen this memorial many times, in many different seasons. But as I came up the small hill this morning, short of breath, the effect of the cemetery's restorative efforts made the scene like something out of Romantic Poetry 101. Spears of sunlight fell onto the memorial through the trees, illuminating the angels that flank the canopy over Charlotte's marble likeness. She stood, forever seventeen, with arms outstretched, like the Virgin Mary. The atmosphere can only be described as religious.

About to make her debut in society, Charlotte was passionate about music and art. She kept pet parrots and, as an amateur artist, had been at work on some sketches for a memorial for her aunt, who had recently died. Those sketches went into her own memorial at Green-Wood, which was commissioned by her grieving father and completed in 1848. Until the monument was finished, Charlotte rested at Saint Patrick's Old Cathedral in Manhattan.

Nearly everything in Charlotte's memorial is symbolic: it is seventeen feet high, seventeen feet long, and adorned by seventeen roses, representing each year of Charlotte's brief life. There are musical instruments and, yes, there were Charlotte's parrots, though 171 years of exposure to the elements have worn them down to little nubs. According to Green-Wood's records, the monument cost Charlotte's father $45,000, over $1 million adjusted for today's inflation.

Just one year after Charlotte died, her fiancé, a young Frenchman named Charles Albert Jarett de la Marie, committed suicide. Because of his romance with Charlotte, their families wanted him to be buried with her, but his death being a suicide prevented him from being buried in consecrated ground. He was laid to rest under a tombstone bearing his family's coat of arms just adjacent to Charlotte's memorial.

There was a time, in the late 1850s, when Charlotte's memorial was one of the most visited places in New York. Visitors could purchase what was known as a carte de visite, an illustration of Charlotte's memorial, and later a photograph, as a record of their visit. Charles Canda, Charlotte's father, had a tablet commissioned with information on her backstory for the curious tourists who filed past for a glimpse. Though its text has worn away with the passage of time, the placard, which still stands, once read: "Charlotte Canda: died suddenly by falling from a carriage on the night of the 3rd of February 1845 being the seventeenth anniversary of her birth day."

The sunny morning when I went to pay homage to Charlotte it was hard to imagine swarming crowds at this memorial or anywhere at Green-Wood. Although every day at Green-Wood is filled with countless stories waiting to be discovered, living visitors are scarce. There might be a passing funeral, or a stray birdwatcher. But Green-Wood Cemetery is gigantic. At 478 acres, it is just slightly smaller than Prospect Park, its neighbor to the north by a few blocks. This puts a considerable amount of space between visitors. In the warmer months, there is the steady hum of Green-Wood's hardworking landscapers. Most of Green-Wood feels and sounds like some kind of outdoor cathedral instead of the center of a vast, bustling metropolis. It is disarmingly quiet.

Green-Wood Cemetery is one of the only places I can go to be completely alone with my thoughts. New Yorkers aren't the

only ones who know the buzzing drone of modern life. No matter the place, we are all well-acquainted with the cold glow of the
smartphone, beckoning from the nightstand when we know we
should be sleeping. And though the Victorians didn't have that
itching feeling in their fingers when the batteries in their electronic

devices died, they certainly needed a break from a rapidly changing world.

The simple explanation of how a place like Green-Wood came into existence is that cities needed a place outside of the city center because their churchyards were overflowing and they were concerned about the spread of disease. In 1832, cholera made landfall in North America, hitting New York City on June 26. Over 3,500 New Yorkers died, and another 80,000 fled the city. But the cemetery was more than just a solution to a sanitation problem. People were also looking for a respite from their daily scramble. And they found it in America's first parks: cemeteries.

Green-Wood's grandeur and beauty creates a sense of amnesia. Just as its founders hoped, I often forget I'm in a cemetery. Passing through the Gothic gates is a transporting experience. As a teenager I was obsessed with Alfred Hitchcock movies and thrilled when I made the pilgrimage to Universal Studios to see the *Psycho* house. Like in the movie, it stands on a hill, but upon closer inspection, the house turns out to be a prop, a facade with nothing behind it. Green-Wood's impressive entrance gates rise, seemingly out of nowhere. Set back from Brooklyn's busy Twenty-Fifth Street, their Gothic design initially brings to mind a giant cathedral—but, like a set piece, they are hollow, only three spires marking the division between the world of the living and the dead.

Green-Wood originally marked its entrance with a humble shack equipped with a bell that would ring any time there was a funeral. But when the cemetery became one of the most popular places to be buried in New York, the neighbors complained about the constant ringing. The imposing entrance gates here today weren't built until 1861. They were designed by Richard Upjohn, who had worked on Trinity Church in Manhattan. By that time, Green-Wood's status afforded it a fancier calling card. The gates include four limestone panels that depict famous scenes from the Bible, with an unsurprising emphasis on eternal life. At the top of the spires, a group of noisy monk parakeets have made their home. No one is exactly sure how the parakeets came to Green-Wood, but legend has it that they escaped from a crate at JFK airport in 1967.

Down the driveway to the right of the gates is a small but ornate chapel, also in the Gothic style. Designed by Warren and Wetmore, the same architectural firm responsible for Grand Central Terminal, Green-Wood's chapel sits at the bottom center of a cul-de-sac, like a rosebud yet to unfold. Like the entrance gates, the chapel presents typical Judeo-Christian signifiers, despite the fact that most park cemeteries were nonsectarian. The religious iconography of many park cemeteries' main structures seems to have been put to use by their founders for lack of a better option. This chapel is a small replica of Christopher Wren's Tom Tower at Oxford's Christ Church College.

The circular drive of the chapel used to be a lake, which was later enlarged and moved to an area directly behind the chapel drive. One of Green-Wood's four lakes, it is called Valley Water,

and in the spring it is wreathed in cherry blossoms. In Japanese culture, *sakura* are thought to look like clouds, floating through the sky—all the petals bloom together in an explosion of fluff and pale pink. Their bursting blooms celebrate the transient nature of life. During one visit to Green-Wood, I sat down for a minute on a bench to take in the splendor of the cherry blossoms. As I watched some turtles sunning themselves on a rock in the water, a soft breeze blew dainty petals into my hair.

Green-Wood was the brainchild of a man named Henry Evelyn Pierrepont. His name might sound familiar to those who've spent time in the borough; Pierrepont Street, in Brooklyn Heights, was named for him. Pierrepont's ideas were focused on what we'd call urban planning. Deeply passionate about community, he became known as Brooklyn's "first citizen." And Pierrepont is buried at Green-Wood, the place he helped build, with the rest of his family. A short stroll from Valley Water leads to the unassuming Pierrepont family plot, at the top of a small hill. In a memorial also designed by Richard Upjohn, Henry's parents are entombed underneath a mini-version of the entrance gates, and Henry himself and other members of his family are interspersed across the top of the mound in freestanding stone crypts. The overall effect looks like an outdoor version of the Chase vault, a mausoleum in Barbados where the urban legend goes that every time the vault was opened to add another member of the family, the coffins inside were found jumbled on the floor in inexplicable disarray.

During Green-Wood's first decade Pierrepont knew he'd need to draw public interest in the cemetery to sell plots. What better way to give Green-Wood some panache than by having a beloved and prominent New Yorker like former senator, mayor, and governor of New York DeWitt Clinton buried there? There was only one problem: Clinton had died with major debts in 1828, and his widow didn't have the means to bury him, much less erect a monument in his memory. Pierrepont offered to move Clinton's body from his friend's mausoleum, where he had been a guest, and had Clinton reinterred in Green-Wood in 1844. An impressive statue of Clinton was installed at City Hall in Manhattan, basically as an advertisement saying, "Come and see me at Green-Wood." Later, the statue was moved atop the grave, where it still stands today.

The top of the Pierrepont hill offers a nice view of the section of the cemetery that includes the resting place of the infamous corrupt politician Boss Tweed and the inventor of the telegraph and Morse code, Samuel Morse. The walk from the entrance gates to the chapel, the lake, and the Pierrepont memorial is an efficient introduction to Green-Wood, and a self-contained mini-history of New York.

Green-Wood's cultural cachet grew rapidly in the years following the Civil War, leading the *New York Times* to write in 1866, "It is the ambition of the New Yorker to live upon Fifth Avenue, to take his airings in the Park and to sleep with his fathers in Green-Wood." The funny thing about this quotation is that without Green-Wood, there would've been no airings in the park because there would've been no park.

As Green-Wood's popularity grew, thanks to its natural beauty, romantic ideals, and celebrity interments, the city took notice. New Yorkers knew "Miss Canda" referred to Charlotte, now a celebrity in the afterlife thanks to her popular memorial at Green-Wood. Urban planners challenged architects to come up with a design for the same sort of green space for Manhattan, and another one for Brooklyn. An architect named Frederick Law Olmsted, with his partner Calvert Vaux, rose to the challenge, and thus Central Park, in 1857, and Prospect Park, in 1867, were born.

Green-Wood was built and designed in a meandering way, partially inspired by the winding footpaths at Mount Auburn, in Cambridge, Massachusetts, America's first park cemetery, itself inspired by Père Lachaise in Paris. But it is also the natural landscape of Green-Wood, formed by glaciers, that gives it the highest point in Brooklyn above sea level: Battle Hill. According to a

New York Times article "How the Ice Age Shaped New York," New York City as a whole was formed by moraines, "a ridge of rubble deposited by an ice age glacier." The biggest moraines were difficult to build on, so that land was left "for parks, cemeteries, and golf courses." This important peak was where, during the Revolutionary War, the English prevailed over the revolutionary forces and gained control of New York Harbor. They may have won the battle, but they didn't win the war, of course.

Any good cemetery historian (and historic cemeteries like Green-Wood often employ one) will explain that park cemeteries were designed to help visitors get lost. There is a reason why the footpaths seem circuitous and it can be difficult to find a way back to an exit. Just ask two friends of mine who wandered into Green-Wood one afternoon, unaware that the cemetery gates close at 5:00 p.m. and found themselves, to their horror, *locked inside the cemetery.* In the midst of Green-Wood, there is so much to take in, I can momentarily forget that I'll need to make my way back out

at some point. The cemetery designers intended this: they wanted Green-Wood to be a place where people could ruminate on their own lives while appreciating Green-Wood's astounding beauty.

The way to explore any cemetery is by foot. Historic cemeteries were planned with this mode of transportation in mind, but even modern-day cemeteries are best explored by walking. (There are of course exceptions to this rule, namely the Forest Lawn cemeteries in Los Angeles and Glendale, California, whose hills are only scalable by the superhuman.) The best thing about walking is discovery. Like exploring a used bookstore or an antiques shop, true treasures are found by accident.

In a historic cemetery like Green-Wood there are many "notable burials" of celebrities and infamous figures from history that make great entries on a Wikipedia page. Making a visit to celebrity graves at any cemetery is one way to be a cemetery explorer. Visitors can pay homage to Leonard Bernstein, DeWitt Clinton, Jean-Michel Basquiat, Henry Steinway, numerous Civil War figures, and gangsters like Bill the Butcher and Albert Anastasia, and see memorials for mass tragedies, like the 1876 Brooklyn Theatre fire.

But the most fascinating stories from Green-Wood are those that I've discovered myself, like the story of Charlotte Canda. Charlotte's memorial at Green-Wood is not a "celebrity" memorial. Not anymore, anyway. She may have become a figure of notoriety in death in the Victorian age, but hardly anyone today has heard her name. I discovered Charlotte's memorial completely by accident, and now every time I visit, it feels like a secret between the two of us. Curators of some of the most famous museums in the world say that even though they've walked the halls hundreds of times they still discover works of art they hadn't noticed before. Like New York City, the sheer magnitude of Green-Wood encourages a constant state of wonder.

When I was young, my family passed a church every single day on our way to school and, really, anytime we left the house.

Every time we drove past the church, and its adjoining cemetery, I wondered about the people who were buried there. The section closest to the church building was the oldest, most likely the resting place of some of the first people who had made a home there, with new burials stretching out across the lawn. These newer graves had most likely been my neighbors. Morbid curiosity is only natural, despite our culture's denial of death.

Historic park cemeteries like Green-Wood are different than modern cemeteries. A new cemetery will be much smaller, due to urban development and the popularity of cremation. I approach new cemeteries with the same curiosity as older ones. But some may find that when death is closer—with today's year on the headstone, for instance—it is more difficult to appreciate the beauty of the cemetery, or its historic import. This is understandable. A new headstone at Green-Wood stops me in my tracks. Some bear an illustration or even a photograph of the deceased. Some of these people have lived short lives. For me, this moment makes my time at the cemetery all the more precious, and instructive. But it is not for everyone. At a historic park cemetery like Green-Wood there is, thankfully, a little more space between you and your inevitable demise.

It is in fact that space, between the living and the dead, that makes Green-Wood such an unusual and important place. Victorians lived much closer to death. Death occurred at home and the deceased was usually laid out in the home's parlor before burial at the churchyard. Hence the name "funeral parlor" and the later change to the term "living room." Life expectancy was much shorter, and illness claimed the lives of many, especially children. According to the research website Our World in Data, in 1860 41.1 percent of the world's newborns would die before they reached their fifth birthday. Death was part of the Victorians' daily life.

Nineteenth-century Americans subscribed to the idea of the Good Death, the idea that with certain parameters in place, death could be both peaceful and meaningful. The tenets of the Good Death included the idea that death would occur at home, with the dying surrounded by loved ones, with ample time to make peace with his or her death and any final pronouncements about his or her life.

As for religious beliefs, by the time Green-Wood was founded in 1838, Christians had shifted from the brutal, vengeful God of the Puritans to a warmer, more loving dogma. Ideas about the afterlife in particular had changed significantly by the nineteenth century. Instead of the idea that illness and/or death were the result of sin for which one would be punished in the afterlife, Christians believed that the afterlife was a reward, death only a transition into a greater eternal life in heaven. The park cemeteries reflect this change in their symbology. Instead of a winged death's head or a reminder that time is running out, like a skull and crossbones, the symbology of the park cemetery is a celebration of life's natural beauty, with flowers, angels, animals, and personal markers of the deceased.

Romantic poetry saw the cemetery as a place not only for deep communion with mortality but for rumination on any number of subjects. Poets like Thomas Gray and John Keats, well-acquainted with death and illness in their own lives, committed their walks through the cemetery to paper, giving us some of the finest poetry ever written. David Charles Sloane, in his epic history of cemeteries in America, *The Last Great Necessity*, explains the importance of the picturesque in rural park cemeteries: "The picturesque offered an opportunity in which nature could be more fully exploited as an instructor about moral and ethical behavior in an increasingly profane and commercial world. The changing seasons reminded visitors of their mortality; the wildness of a thunderstorm, of their vulnerability; and nature's aura, of their insignificance."

As I was taking photographs of Battle Hill one afternoon, I walked down the path and came across a compact mausoleum built into the hillside. Its design included the flying hourglass, reminding me that *tempus fugit*. The dark, weathered stone of the mausoleum stood in stark contrast to the bright blue sky peeking out from underbrush of dark green leaves. A spray of violets seemed to look up from the foot of the mausoleum steps, a shy, smiling greeting.

Pierrepont chose the cemetery's name with good intentions, stating it should "always remain a scene of rural quiet and beauty and leafiness." It has lived up to all three of these elements. According to the New York City Audubon, Green-Wood's unique ecosystem (with four lakes) makes it ideal for numerous species of birds, including those incredibly rare, making it a haven for birdwatchers. "Tombstones and monuments act as perches for late fall bluebirds," Audubon points out. "The old burial grounds, low and grassy, attract resident Red-tailed Hawk and Eastern Meadowlark. Cemetery workers keep track of the Red-tailed Hawk and can point out their whereabouts."

The cemetery contains more than 7,000 trees, 172 different species and 76 genera. There are 182 living American beech trees. Green-Wood was recently given the accreditation of a Level III Arboretum. Another favorite mausoleum of mine, embedded in a hill, is flanked at its top by a large beech tree whose roots seem to melt down the slope surrounding the tomb in a loving embrace.

One of Green-Wood's most famous trees, though, appropriately, is dead. Behind the hard-to-find gravestone of artist Jean-Michel Basquiat, there is an enormous tree stump covered with repetitions of his signature tag: a small crown. No one is certain about the crown's origins, though his father said it signified that he was descended from royalty.

Basquiat's is one of the most visited graves at Green-Wood. When I went to visit him, I was surprised to find him buried in a long line of small tombstones of mostly Italian American families. His simple tombstone was adorned by mementos from visitors paying their respects. They had left him paintbrushes, writing implements, Polaroids, guitar picks, vodka bottles, and, on that particular sunny day, a colorful pinwheel. Perhaps finding his resting place humble in view of his popularity, fans have migrated toward the huge tree stump as an extension of their pilgrimage, marking it with his signature crown.

Basquiat was born and raised in Brooklyn, not far from Green-Wood. In one of his paintings, *Bird on Money*, there are the words "Green Wood" painted in the bottom left corner. After he left Brooklyn as a young man, his work put him on the path to

stardom before he died of a drug overdose at the age of twenty-seven in 1988. His father, who no longer lived in Brooklyn but was familiar with Green-Wood as a former resident of the borough, went to the cemetery to bury his son. At the time, no one working in the cemetery was familiar with his work, and his father purchased a reasonable stone for him in a long line of graves. In 2017 one of his paintings earned $110.5 million at Sotheby's, the highest sale of any work by an American artist. At Green-Wood, his epitaph simply reads, "Artist."

His makeshift monument, in the form of a tree stump, is one of the most unique sights at Green-Wood. Its presence, along with the many souvenirs and tchotchkes left at Basquiat's gravesite, is symbolic of the lasting impression an artist's work can leave on one's life. The DIY aspect of the tree stump makes Basquiat's legacy all the more poignant.

As I was headed out of the cemetery that afternoon, I stepped away from Basquiat's grave to investigate others in the area. I was immediately met with several groups of people asking for directions to Basquiat's grave. It was obvious it was their first trip to Green-Wood. One couple told me it was their first trip to New York (they were from Paris) and that Green-Wood had been at the top of their list of places to visit. I watched with a smile from afar as the

separate groups politely made time for each other at the gravesite, snapping pictures and going to investigate the stump. One woman quietly kneeled and placed her hands on the stone itself.

It's fascinating to view New York City from the hills of Green-Wood. Battle Hill, the highest natural point in all of Brooklyn, was prime for spotting the ongoing enemy attacks on New York Harbor during the Revolutionary War. Through the trees lies the harbor in the distance, with Lower Manhattan marked by the lonely Freedom Tower. There is a monument to the soldiers who fought to preserve the Union during the Civil War, and a statue of Minerva, or Athena, the goddess of war. Minerva raises her hand in salute to another protective figure across the harbor—the Statue of Liberty.

These striking views of Manhattan are unique to Green-Wood. I like to compare the same view from the top of the hill with historical imagery over the years to see how New York has changed. Though Manhattan is practically a game of Tetris, constantly changing, it's fascinating how the harbor looks pretty much the same, though sometimes, while living in New York, I would forget it is an island.

Because it is so large, Green-Wood is flanked by a total of six distinct Brooklyn neighborhoods, beginning with Green-Wood Heights, where the main entrance gates are located. Park Slope to the north and Windsor Terrace to the northeast both border Prospect Park. These are gentrified neighborhoods, mostly due to the proximity to the subway and the park, which contains the Prospect Park Zoo and the Brooklyn Botanic Garden. Just below Green-Wood Heights there is Sunset Park, made up of a majority of Puerto Ricans, Mexicans, and other Hispanic residents. Green-Wood's southeastern entrance at the Fort Hamilton Gatehouse spills out into Kensington, an incredibly diverse neighborhood of immigrants, and Borough Park, home to one of the largest communities of Orthodox Jews outside of Israel. Brooklyn is New

York City's most populous borough. To get a sense of just how large and diverse it is, enter the cemetery through one neighborhood and exit to another. A walk through Green-Wood can feel like traveling to a different continent.

As the progenitor of Central Park and Prospect Park, it's no surprise that Green-Wood has much to offer in the ways of natural beauty. The botanical gardens in the Bronx and in Brooklyn

both owe a lot to Green-Wood. But there's still something Green-Wood has over the parks and the gardens: peace. Central Park is busy. The Brooklyn Botanic Garden, especially on a nice spring day, is positively mobbed with people. Admission is expensive, and it is crowded and loud. Green-Wood offers just as much natural beauty, if not more. There is no price of admission. And it is quiet. Given the fact that the population of Brooklyn has increased fifty-fold since Green-Wood's first burial in 1840, the fact that it still offers this kind of natural beauty in completely meditative space is nothing short of a miracle.

In addition to sweeping landscapes, like its lakes, terraced walkways with mausoleums crouched like little houses, gorgeous foliage in the spring (including explosive cherry blossoms), and architectural feats like the entrance gates and the chapel, Green-Wood is also a place where one comes face-to-face with the inevitable. "Visitors were thought to enter the cemetery in a state of anxiety and ambition and to leave calm and contemplative," Sloane writes in *The Last Great Necessity*. "They would feel a renewed respect for the dead and be reminded of human frailty." One of my favorite headstones at Green-Wood belongs to Herman and Elizabeth Aldrich. Resting atop their shared stone is a harvested bundle of wheat. In Christian symbolism of the day, wheat represented a long life, usually more than seventy years. Herman died at seventy-nine and Elizabeth at eighty-three. It's a bit of a relief to see the wheat symbol in a park cemetery, rather than the lamb, which represents the loss of a young child or an infant, or a rose, which symbolizes the death of a young girl.

Why aren't cemeteries still like this? Long story short, the Civil War changed everything about death in America. Those long four years made the tenets of the Good Death impossible to achieve: soldiers died far from home, and their bodies were rarely recovered. There was no opportunity for reflection or last words. Also, the United States was dealing with a loss of life of epic proportions. The need for municipal cemeteries, controlled and financed by the government, arose. Things like embalming came into practice. There was little time for meditation or romanticism. One could write an entire book about this fascinating history, and, in fact, someone has. For further reading, look to Drew Gilpin Faust's excellent book *The Republic of Suffering: Death and the American Civil War.*

Civil War–specific history buffs will find plenty of related stories at Green-Wood, including the Civil War monument on Battle Hill. In 2015 the cemetery launched the Civil War project to identify all of the Civil War veterans who rest at Green-Wood. So far, the number is 3,300. Two of the most notable are the Prentiss brothers, who died after fighting on opposite sides in Petersburg, Virginia, on April 2, 1865.

Clifton and William were from the border state of Maryland. Clifton chose to fight to secure the Union while his younger brother William chose to join the Confederacy. They were both wounded and, as the story goes, William begged to see his brother and the two were reunited on the battlefield. William was attended to in the hospital by none other than Walt Whitman, who recorded their story. William died in the hospital in June, and though Clifton had gone home to recuperate, he died in August. The two rest at Green-Wood, just adjacent to the chapel overlooking Valley Water, side by side for eternity.

The Civil War changed not only death in America, but nearly everything about American life. As the North became the center of industry and the South foundered in the wake of its defeat and the beginnings of Reconstruction, a wealthy, elite class emerged in New York City. And those with money wanted their endings to be as grand as their lifestyle.

After the Civil War, the mausoleum, rather than traditional burial, grew in popularity. The word "mausoleum" comes from the name of one of the fourth-century BC kings of Caria who built a small house for his mortal remains. The finest early examples of mausoleums are the pyramids, built for the pharaohs of Egypt. At

Green-Wood and other park cemeteries in the United States, your monument in death was another way to show your wealth and success in life.

At Green-Wood's entrance there is a cluster of mausoleums nestled into the terraced path above the receiving vault to the left of the chapel. The receiving tomb or vault, by the way, was like a catchall mausoleum for any person being interred in Green-Wood. A body would be "received" into this crypt until its permanent lodgings became available. The mausoleums above the receiving tomb are not freestanding, making their front doors the only hope for a peek inside.

Mausoleums look like little houses. When I was in college, I used to walk home from class through the residential area, where mostly professors lived, close to campus, in adorable ranch-style homes. These small houses were always beautifully decorated, well-kept, filled with books, and sometimes had fireplaces. They looked so warm and inviting in the Midwestern winter; it was difficult to keep my curiosity at bay as a lonely college student. I

would peek inside and wonder about the inhabitants. Not much has changed.

In a park cemetery there will be a plethora of gorgeous mausoleums whose designs present a condensed history of architectural styles in America. Egyptian Revival was all the rage during the Art Deco period of the early 1900s, thanks to the discovery of King Tut's tomb in 1922, so it's very common to see mausoleums with Egyptian motifs, like scarabs, ankhs, birds, and more around this time. But Green-Wood has one of the finest examples of this fad in the Van Ness Parsons mausoleum, which blends Art Deco–Egyptian Revival style with Christian symbolism.

The Van Ness Parsons mausoleum is hard to miss. First of all, it's a pyramid. Perplexingly, Jesus Christ himself greets visitors at its entrance, holding a lamb, joined by Jochebed holding baby Moses, or Mary holding the baby version of Jesus, depending on interpretation. To Jesus's right there's another female figure holding a baby, which probably represents Pharaoh's wife finding baby

Moses. A friendly sphinx looks up at Mary, like a family pet, and above the doorway there are Egyptian vulture wings, which symbolize maternity.

The owner and occupant of the mausoleum was Alfred Ross Parsons, a pianist and music teacher who was also a dedicated Egyptologist. He wrote a book, *New Light from the Great Pyramid*, on the astronomical and geographical discoveries of the Egyptians. Parsons died in 1933. His wife, Alice Schuyler Van Ness, predeceased him in 1931 and also rests in the mausoleum.

Green-Wood hosts an occasional "open house" on select weekends when they will open certain mausoleums (which are always locked, of course) to visitors on a scheduled tour. I have long wondered about what the interior of the Van Ness Parsons mausoleum must look like, and asked the helpful powers that be at Green-Wood if they would open it. Alas, it is still an active mausoleum, meaning the family members still own it and intend on using it for future entombments. And that means, sadly, it is not open to the public.

Perhaps it's because they remind me of little houses, or that they are perfect bite-sized boxes of architecture, but I have a deep love for mausoleums. There are multitudes to discover at Green-Wood, including the Steinway mausoleum, which houses the remains of Henry E. Steinway Jr., the founder of Steinway & Sons pianos. This mausoleum is Green-Wood's largest, with room for 256 people. No word on whether those vacancies are for sale.

The Niblo mausoleum, built into the hills surrounding Crescent Water Lake, is one of the prettiest sights at Green-Wood. Protected by two rather perturbed-looking lions, William Niblo's legacy at Green-Wood is rather scandalous. As the mausoleum was paid for and completed well before Niblo's death (in 1878), the theater impresario hosted parties on the lawn in front of his future tomb that featured bare-legged dancers and other off-color entertainment for the era, much to the chagrin of the cemetery's management. Today, Green-Wood has embraced Niblo's legacy by throwing similar soirees for visitors, with entertainment like tight-rope walkers, live music, and even fire dancers.

No one epitomized the rise of this elite class of New Yorkers better than a man named Ward McAllister, New York's original gossip girl. In the late 1800s, McAllister became the self-appointed "arbiter of New York society." In other words, he decided who mattered in the lifestyles of the rich and richer. Through a sketchy connection to the Astors and his wife's wealth, McAllister's exploits with the upper crust resulted in the creation of what he called "the Four Hundred," a list of the most fashionable people in New York society. Eventually, he published the full list of names in the *New York Times* on February 16, 1892.

After a lifetime of snobbery, McAllister went too far with the publication of a tell-all book, *Society As I Have Found It*, in 1890. The Astors and other wealthy New York elites were not happy about it, and McAllister was blacklisted from society life. He spent his last five years in disgrace and died, tragically, eating dinner alone. His funeral was quite the sideshow, receiving a write-up in the paper of record that described the frenzy for souvenirs. "A noticeable and regrettable feature of the services at the church was the indecent scramble for the wreaths and loose flowers made by many of the women present," the reporter wrote. "One woman had to be threatened with arrest before she would give up a wreath that she had appropriated."

Everyone who was anyone in New York society would have wanted to be buried at Green-Wood Cemetery. Ward McAllister *is* entombed at Green-Wood, but he isn't buried in a lavish family mausoleum. No, McAllister was committed for eternity to the Green-Wood's catacombs, a freestanding crypt—the apartment building version of communal burial—in shame. Constructed in the 1850s into a hillside, Green-Wood's catacombs were built in a need for more space as an offering to those who wanted indoor interment like a mausoleum but couldn't afford it. The catacombs are normally closed to the public, though Green-Wood opens them frequently today for special events and performances. It's ironic that McAllister, the self-appointed arbiter of New York society, ended up in the one section of Green-Wood where he would be easily forgotten.

I was lucky enough to gain entry to the catacombs on a hot afternoon in May. Despite the rising temperatures outside, inside it was freezing. Every breath I took became visible. These are not

luxury entombments—there were stray leaves, cobwebs, crumbling crypt facades. As I approached Ward McAllister's family room, his bronze placard glittered green in the light of my phone. I realized that his marker, like all the surfaces in the catacombs, was covered in beaded moisture.

Even those who had paid top dollar to spend eternity in a lavish mausoleum were, over time, just as easily forgotten. As the twentieth century raged on, cemeteries in America fell into disrepair, out of sight, out of mind. New Yorkers now had actual parks for green space, inspired by rural cemeteries like Green-Wood. They didn't need the cemetery as a form of recreation, and cemeteries became more isolated. An increase in embalming and the funeral home (with on-site mortuary) led to the sterilization of death in American culture. With major advancements in medicine, by the 1970s there was nearly a complete denial of death in American culture. By then, most people died in hospitals or hospice care, and today they still do. A lack of space, environmental concerns, and the expense of a modern funeral has made cremation the most popular choice for Americans. In a sense, cemeteries are obsolete.

New York City had also gone through a serious change. Cemetery vandalism was rampant, and the idea of the Good Death was far from anyone's mind. "If you approached the cemetery gates with anything other than a bouquet of flowers you would be turned away," Green-Wood Cemetery president Richard J. Moylan told the *New York Times* about the dark period before Green-Wood's social rejuvenation. Gates were locked. To this day, when I tell people about going to visit a cemetery, most respond in astonishment, "You just . . . walk in?"

When Moylan took over stewardship of Green-Wood in 1986 (working his way up through the ranks after starting out as a member of the lawn maintenance crew in 1972, when his father worked at the cemetery) the idea of drawing more living people into the cemetery was at first a financial necessity. There is a great deal of reportage in the *New York Times*'s archive on Green-Wood's annual fundraising party and several notable New Yorkers, like novelists Paul Auster and Siri Hustvedt, who have championed the cemetery and its importance by planning on being buried there. Actor John Turturro, Jesus of *The Big Lebowski*, appears as host in a promotional video the cemetery shot in 2014.

But just as Green-Wood was working to secure its place in the modern, digital world, it took two serious blows, back-to-back. In August 2012, the cemetery was vandalized. Forty-three memorials were damaged. Aside from pushing over gravestones and other markers and smashing them into pieces, the criminal(s) went to the trouble of scratching the porcelain photographs of the deceased on some tombstones. "I have been visiting Green-Wood since 1986," cemetery historian Jeff Richman wrote on Green-Wood's blog. "While I recall some incidents of vandalism, I cannot remember anything on this scale or close to it." Devastatingly, the person or persons responsible for this disgusting crime have never been brought to justice.

With the cemetery still reeling from the vandalism, on October 29, 2012, Hurricane Sandy blew through New York and Green-Wood's 478 acres, destroying three hundred trees and damaging two hundred monuments. Groundskeepers later estimated it took months to clear the roads of debris and a full year for the cemetery to complete its cleanup. Because Green-Wood is made up of the dead, not the living, administrators discovered that the site wasn't eligible for FEMA aid. Thankfully, in 2015, Governor Cuomo allocated several million dollars to the Parks Department for the cleanup and reconstruction of several historical sites, including Green-Wood, which was hit the hardest.

In the wake of Hurricane Sandy, high school students from North Brooklyn chipped in with some of the repairs. With over 560,000 permanent residents, keeping Green-Wood green and safe is no small task. In 2016, the cemetery was registered as a National Historic Landmark, which undoubtedly helps to protect its important heritage. In 2017, Green-Wood hired preservationist Neela Wickremesinghe, whose three-person crew is responsible for Green-Wood's neediest restoration cases.

Green-Wood's events program gets back to the roots of the park cemetery movement, which intended cemeteries to be more for the living than the dead. At Green-Wood today, visitors are encouraged to walk with or without a tour guide, to take photographs, and to attend events. The cemetery has even partnered with the travel website Atlas Obscura and the former Morbid Anatomy Museum to host exhibits on death culture and history and performances featuring live music and interactive theater.

Green-Wood's return to original intentions of the park cemetery movement is part of a broader cultural return to the idea of the Good Death. Today, it's known as the Death Positive movement, one that encourages people and society to be open about death and dying in hopes that an acknowledgment and discussion of our inevitable demise will lead us to what nineteenth-century

Americans recognized as the Good Death. For modern-day Americans, that means establishing a living will and advanced directive, being responsible about making provisions for your remains, and researching options like home funerals and green burial. In other words, being unafraid to confront death should

enable us to make important decisions about our deaths, saving surviving loved ones from despairing decisions in a chaotic time.

In his wonderful piece about the redeeming nature of cemeteries, "Mr. Hunter's Grave," originally published in the *New Yorker* on September 14, 1956, Joseph Mitchell claimed, "For some reason I don't know and don't want to know, after I have spent an hour or so in one of these cemeteries . . . my spirits lift, I become quite cheerful, and then I go for a long walk." The rise in spirit Mitchell describes but can't make sense of is the result of the charms of the park cemetery, which blends all the natural beauty of a park with a gentle reminder that life is short. Different parts of the cemetery speak to its visitors in different ways depending on the circumstances. One unseasonably warm day in January I arrived at Green-Wood, depressed and brooding. I walked in a part of the cemetery I had never been through before, sweating through my coat in one of those "what for" moods. As I approached a hillside, the sun broke through the clouds and it started to rain. I left the cemetery that day in search of a better way of being.

Nearly every major city in the United States contains at least one historic park cemetery. America's first, Mount Auburn, is a must-visit. But even Mount Auburn doesn't have the magical quality that Green-Wood holds for me, likely because Green-Wood was my first park cemetery. The cemeteries I visited growing up either were attached to a churchyard or were depressing memorial parks with yellow grass and flat, invisible stones. A walk through the park, especially in an urban setting, can be a soothing balm, and we have Green-Wood Cemetery to thank for these urban oases in New York City. When I leave Green-Wood, it always feels like a little loss. To step into the noise and traffic of Brooklyn, to figure out my commute back to the responsibilities of home, the demands of work, is jarring after time spent in this safe haven. But it's this juxtaposition that makes Green-Wood's existence in the midst of the most crowded city in America all the more important.

Many would call a walk in the cemetery morbid, and they aren't wrong. But in a place like Green-Wood, you don't confront your mortality like an enemy, the way we inevitably do when we lose a loved one, or when we're caring for the ill, or when we're sick ourselves. In Green-Wood, death walks right beside you. Surprisingly, it makes a great companion.

PRESBYTERIANS AND PAGANS ALIKE

WOODLAWN CEMETERY, THE BRONX

After a long, hot afternoon at Woodlawn Cemetery, I made my way back to the gates to exit. I stumbled upon what I initially thought must have been the cemetery's chapel, a large Gothic structure with bronze spires, stained-glass windows, and gargoyles. This is indeed a chapel—but it doesn't belong to Woodlawn. This gorgeous mausoleum is the tomb of Alva and Oliver Belmont.

Alva Belmont was what you might call a formidable woman. Born in Mobile, Alabama, to a commission merchant and the daughter of a US congressman, Alva summered with her family in Rhode Island. She married William Vanderbilt, then did the unthinkable in New York society when she divorced him in 1895 (he was notoriously unfaithful) and married his friend, the even wealthier Oliver Belmont, a congressman and founder of Belmont Raceway. But Alva's second marriage would last only twelve years. Oliver died of appendicitis in 1908, and Alva almost immediately set upon her plans for his ornate tomb at Woodlawn.

Designed by the architecture firm Hunt & Hunt, the Belmont mausoleum is a near-perfect replica of the Chapel Saint Hubert in France, designed by Leonardo da Vinci. Da Vinci spent the last three years of his life as a guest of King François I. When da Vinci died in 1519, his body was placed in the chapel in which he had been hard at work. Since the chapel was sacked during the French Revolution, it remains unclear whether da Vinci still resides there.

Despite the fact that Oliver was not a religious man, the Belmont mausoleum boasts an elaborate frieze above its doors that depicts the stag that supposedly convinced Saint Hubert to convert to Christianity, a crucifix rising from its horns like a crown. Surrounded by animals in an abundant forest scene, the panel looks like a Renaissance tapestry. Above that, the Virgin and child are flanked by Charles VIII of France and his wife, Anne of Brittany, kneeling in respect. The frieze's white stone stands out next to the weathered Indiana limestone of the rest of the mausoleum. It practically glows.

After Oliver's death, Alva became a dedicated suffragist, donating large sums of money and real estate to help the cause. She worked to enfranchise and empower women of color to fight for the right to vote, at a time when suffrage was seen as the battle of white, upper-class women. Once the right to vote was won in 1920, Alva lived mostly in Europe. There, she could be closer to her daughter, Consuelo Vanderbilt, who had been pressured (by Alva!) into an unhappy marriage with the Duke of Marlborough.

All the while Alva kept a watchful eye on her mausoleum, which she called "my chapel," at Woodlawn. She insisted that the mausoleum be opened to the public on "every pleasant afternoon." When the chapel's caretaker fell ill in 1917 and his wife offered to monitor the chapel in his stead, Alva wrote to Woodlawn explaining the situation with a postscript: "I am taking it for granted that this woman is as respectable and trustworthy as her husband. If you know anything to the contrary will you kindly advise me."

Some of the stationery on which Alva wrote her correspondence to Woodlawn was emblazoned with the motto "Votes for Women."

When Alva died in Paris in 1933, she was brought back to New York for a crowded funeral in which all of the pallbearers were female. Not bad for a girl from Mobile, Alabama. She was laid to rest in her chapel next to Oliver. The suffragist banner that she carried was buried with her and now hangs in the mausoleum. It reads, "Failure is impossible."

Though I lived in New York City for over a decade, my first visit to the Bronx coincided with my first visit to Woodlawn Cemetery. Not knowing much about the borough myself, I asked some fellow New Yorkers to tell me what came to mind when they thought of the Bronx. The replies varied from the expected ("dangerous") to the socially conscious ("poor," "disenfranchised") to the honest: "I have no idea what the Bronx is," one said. "It's a complete void."

For *New York* magazine, Bronx native Benjamin Wallace-Wells writes that the Bronx is both "elusive and placid." He argues that while other boroughs like Brooklyn or even states like New Jersey have worked hard to differentiate themselves from Manhattan, the Bronx has held on, ambivalently attached to the city like a phantom limb.

The impression that the Bronx is a blank slate could stem from the fact that when Woodlawn Cemetery was founded, in 1863 during the Civil War, that's exactly what it was: empty former farmland, convenient to Manhattan, a great location for a cemetery. Unlike Green-Wood, which required passage over the East River, grieving families could hire a funeral train up to Woodlawn, right at the end of the line, and be back in midtown Manhattan in time for dinner.

Today, the Bronx *is* dangerous—there is more violent crime committed here than in the city as a whole. It *is* disenfranchised—out of every 100,000 residents, 577 are incarcerated, higher than the city as a whole. Twenty-two percent of the Bronx's residents live below the poverty line, and the average annual household income is $48,012. But the Bronx is anything but a void. Inside its borders lies a vast and permanent chronicle of New York City itself. The mark of a true New Yorker is an obsession with location. So much of a New Yorker's day-to-day existence is defined by the neighborhood in which he or she resides: everything from access to the subway to proximity to work, to the park, to good schools, to chic restaurants. Traveling from basically anywhere in New York City to Woodlawn reveals the New Yorker's reliance on the subway. It is the last stop on the uptown 4 train. The journey from Grand Central Station at Forty-Second Street to Woodlawn can feel downright epic.

Most commuters on the 4 train are probably going to Yankee Stadium for a ball game. They get off the train at 161st Street, leaving the rest of the commuters on their way to the actual Bronx. It was obvious one Saturday afternoon on my way to Woodlawn that the other people on the train were coming from work. They were dressed in hospital scrubs; they were couriers carrying packages. One deliveryman fell from his bicycle as he dozed off, inciting concern from other passengers.

Though the trip is long—coming from north Brooklyn, it usually takes just over an hour to reach Woodlawn—I don't mind the lengthy commute. For one thing, the 4 train goes aboveground at 125th Street. The view, elevated over the streets of the Bronx, serves as a reminder of the sheer expansiveness of the city, each of its boroughs containing multitudes: neighborhoods, people, and communities. Also, after being underground for so long, it's nice to see the sun.

"Last stop, everybody off," the conductor announces when the train has reached the Woodlawn station, which is named for the cemetery. There are usually several drivers standing at the bottom of the stairs asking if anyone needs a ride. They always seem surprised when I shake my head no, walk over the crosswalk, and stride directly into the cemetery.

Woodlawn's entrance gates are not large or impressive. They don't need to be: the impressive stuff is inside.

Unlike Green-Wood, whose meandering pathways encourage visitors to get lost, Woodlawn was developed on the "landscape lawn plan." This means that plots and sections were opened up one by one as they were sold. The result is a segmented cemetery that, though very different from the layout and goals of rural park cemeteries, unfolds like the unique neighborhoods of New York City.

The prime real estate is at the front of the cemetery. Woodlawn's Central Avenue is the mausoleum version of Fifth Avenue. The families that built these mausoleums are mostly the same families that owned those houses on Fifth Avenue, families who built New York City and whose heirs cashed in on their astounding industry in devastating and desperate ways. As Susan Olsen, Woodlawn's historian, put it, "The people who made the money in New York are buried at Green-Wood. The people who spent it are here at Woodlawn."

In the first few pages of Edith Wharton's juicy novel of Gilded Age New York, *The Custom of the Country*, a new suitor appears on social-climber Undine Spragg's radar. She asks a family friend if his background is "stylish." When the friend replies that his family (with their extended relatives) lives on Washington Square in Lower Manhattan, Undine, scandalized, responds, "'Way down there? Why do they live with somebody else? Haven't they got the means to have a home of their own?" Living anywhere but on Fifth Avenue meant you were, plainly, a nobody.

The mausoleum as a sign of wealth and prestige is not a new concept. But at Woodlawn, which boasts 1,352 private mausoleums, the most in the country, the showmanship of the wealthy people who are buried there is simply at another level.

The spectacular mausoleum of Frank Winfield Woolworth, founder of the five-and-dime discount store empire, acts as Woodlawn's greeter. At the time of his death in 1919, Woolworth was worth $76.5 million. His ornate Egyptian Revival mausoleum at

Woodlawn is protected by two big-breasted Greek sphinx. (As it turns out, Egyptian sphinx are male.) This mausoleum has the largest lot in the cemetery, at one-third of an acre.

The most infamous permanent resident in the Woolworth mausoleum, though, is not Frank. It is America's "poor little rich girl," Woolworth's granddaughter, Barbara Hutton, who inherited one-third of his estate. During her lifetime she was one of the richest women in the world. But as the adage goes, money can't buy you happiness, and Hutton's life was marred by a series of bad marriages (seven, including one with Cary Grant) and tragedy (the loss of her only son in a plane crash). One society columnist who covered Hutton's fifth wedding scathingly reported that the bride "wore black and carried a scotch-and-soda."

Hutton, whose mother likely died from suicide, claimed all her marital problems stemmed from loneliness and died at the age of sixty-six in Beverly Hills, suffering from complications from anorexia. It was rumored she had burned through all her money. Whatever her financial status at the time of her death, she was entombed with her mother, her grandparents, and her beloved son in the Woolworth mausoleum at Woodlawn.

Woodlawn's epic mausoleums were back in the news in 2011 with the death of Huguette Clark, another "poor little rich girl" who had morphed into a reclusive heiress. Clark was the daughter of industrialist William A. Clark. Huguette's beloved sister Andrée

died at age sixteen of spinal meningitis and her half brother Paul also died young of a bacterial infection. By the time her father died in 1907, Huguette was tragically well-acquainted with the family mausoleum at Woodlawn.

She lived a rather nomadic life until the death of her mother in 1963. Afterward, she rarely ventured outside and checked herself into Beth Israel Hospital, where she lived for twenty-two years, paying exorbitant and probably completely unnecessary medical bills. She arranged for a weekly delivery of flowers to the family mausoleum at Woodlawn.

Olsen, Woodlawn's historian, was surprised to learn in 2011 that not only was Huguette still alive, but she planned on being buried in her family tomb. Technically, the mausoleum was full. But Huguette wanted what she wanted, and she had the funds. So Woodlawn made a "special accommodation" for the reclusive heiress, drilling into the side of the mausoleum to find space for her casket.

When Huguette died later that year, because of her eccentric life story, the New York press (in particular the *New York Post*) was eager to catch a glimpse of Huguette's burial at Woodlawn. Frank E. Campbell, the storied New York funeral home, had made a copper casket (Huguette's father was known as "the copper king") especially for her. But Woodlawn was intent on honoring Huguette's need for privacy. They entombed her with her family very early in the morning, before the gates of the cemetery had opened, and the press completely missed out.

Despite its ostensibly more organized "landscape lawn plan," I still got lost during my last visit to Woodlawn trying to locate the Harbeck mausoleum, the largest in the cemetery. Based on my map, I knew it was just adjacent to the Woolworth mausoleum. One would think by now I'd be adept at reading cemetery maps, but I meandered aimlessly for a good twenty minutes before a Woodlawn volunteer in a golf cart took pity on me and asked if I needed help.

It was a bustling day at the cemetery, and Bruce, a volunteer, explained that Woodlawn volunteers were hard at work placing flags at every veteran's grave in the cemetery in honor of Memorial Day. Despite this large undertaking, Bruce offered to drop me by the Harbeck mausoleum and gave me his cell phone number in case I needed another ride during my visit.

I had indeed been walking in the completely wrong direction on my way to find the Harbeck mausoleum. As Bruce and I zipped around the correct corner, the cathedral-style tomb rose from behind the trees, perched atop its own island in the middle of a circular drive.

"Wow," I said.

"Yup," Bruce replied.

I had seen plenty of photographs of the Harbeck mausoleum. But seeing it in person is something else entirely.

When John Harbeck met and fell in love with young telegraph operator Kate Hammel in the late 1870s, there was just one problem. He was (technically) already married. Luckily for John and Kate, however, his first "marriage" had never been legal. That didn't stop his first wife from suing. She lost, and John and Kate went on to make quite the life for themselves in both New York City and Boulder, Colorado. Their mansion home once housed the Boulder History Museum from 1985 to 2018.

The plan was eventually for the Harbecks to establish residency in Paris. They had already purchased tickets for passage when John caught pneumonia and died at the Plaza Hotel on November 8, 1910. Kate had quite the legal debacle on her hands in terms of which state, Colorado or New York, could claim the tax on John's estate. In the end, Colorado won and collected $100,000.

Despite the tax, Kate was left with a sizable inheritance at her husband's death. A big chunk of it went to the creation of their family mausoleum at Woodlawn. The cathedral-style mausoleum took eight years to complete and boasts three Tiffany stained-glass windows. It is the only mausoleum at Woodlawn (and maybe in history) to be wired for electricity. Kate made this unusual request, and Woodlawn obliged—though the electricity was never turned on.

Kate herself decided to stay in New York at the Plaza, and most of her correspondence to Woodlawn about the mausoleum is written on impressive Plaza Hotel stationery. Tragically, she died on New Year's Eve 1930 after a bizarre accident at her makeshift home. Accounts vary, but apparently Kate was caught (or crushed) in the revolving doors at the Plaza, suffered a broken hip, and died. At the time of her death, her estate was still worth nearly $7 million.

As I walked around the mausoleum, snapping pictures of its windows and the gargoyles that protect it, there was the sudden and inexplicable sound of gunshots. I jumped out of my skin before realizing I wasn't far from Woodlawn's chapel, where, to be sure, there was a military funeral under way. It was the honor guard's salute I'd heard. As I walked by, the group of them, white-gloved, gave me a somber nod.

Families who planned the ultimate in eternal resting places, mausoleums, were not only building the structure and all the embellishments that went with it. In the landscape lawn design, they were also planning a vast "mini-estate." In addition to their personal architect, families would also partner with a landscape designer to select the flora around the mausoleum. "The planting was planned to both emphasize the structure's scale and, at least partially, to screen out the neighboring mausoleums," Andrew Scott Dolkart explains about the Woolworth mausoleum's massive lot, in *Sylvan Cemetery: Architecture, Art and Landscape at Woodlawn*.

There's one mausoleum that perfectly illustrates the importance of garden design at Woodlawn, and it's just a short walk behind the Harbeck site. Though you wouldn't call it understated, it's one of the most charming and serene tombs in the cemetery.

Like the Harbeck mausoleum, the Harkness mausoleum occupies its own circular lot in the center of a drive, surrounded by other, smaller mausoleums. It looks like a small English chapel, complete with stairs and an entrance gate. As I approached the gate on the small footpath, the scene was nothing short of idyllic: there were dogwoods and beautiful plantings. The blue sky and chirping birds only added to the sense of being in a meditative garden.

Edward and Mary Harkness were both dedicated philanthropists. Born into wealth, Edward had been an inheritor of Standard Oil, and the couple made major donations (money and buildings) to places like Yale and Harvard, New York Presbyterian Hospital, the Metropolitan Museum, and many more. They had a long and fruitful relationship with architect James Gamble Rogers, whom they asked to design their mausoleum at Woodlawn. Beatrix Farrand, one of America's most distinguished garden designers and a family friend, did the landscape design.

In 1921, when they were both forty-seven, Edward and Mary bought a lot at Woodlawn. But Rogers wasn't happy with

the location and suggested a different one. Hoping to avoid the ostentatious and predictable boxy shape of most mausoleums, he embarked on a sunken chapel with entryway and surrounding gardens. The mausoleum was completed in 1925. Edward died and was entombed there in 1940, and Mary joined him ten years later. Thanks to committed funds from the family, the structure and grounds underwent a full restoration, completed in 2012, making the Harkness mausoleum one of the mausoleums at Woodlawn that most closely resembles its creators' original vision.

Scholars and students hoping to research the history of landscape design and architecture will find a plethora of fascinating examples at Woodlawn. This relationship between the architect and commissioner is rare in today's society. In Woodlawn's heyday, it was typical for a man to have an architect design his city apartment and country houses, and a landscape designer for the gardens. Then the team would come together to design the ultimate project: the final resting place.

This sort of collaboration is a delight for those passionate about the history of architecture and design. Woodlawn has given all of its records, with all the blueprints, sketches, and correspondence between the lot/mausoleum owners and their designers, to Columbia University. The remarkable archive, over nine thousand feet of paper, resides at the Avery Architectural and Fine Arts Library.

Landscape design was one of the few professions "acceptable" for women at the turn of the century in New York. Most women would have to reconcile their passion for design with private projects, like the residences of society families. But Farrand defined the practice of landscape design in America. She had many projects at Woodlawn and, in fact, her influence is felt all over the United States.

Thanks to family connections (Farrand was the niece of Edith Wharton and a good friend of Henry James), Farrand was able to pursue public projects unavailable to others. At Woodlawn, perhaps her two largest projects were the Milliken family plot and the

Harkness mausoleum. "Well known for her strict requirement that her landscapes be maintained," Farrand made a habit of "visiting the site itself and sending notes to the cemetery's superintendent suggesting pruning, watering and thinning," writes Dolkart. "Farrand's continuing attention and the interest of the Milliken family may explain why at least some aspects of this landscape survive, while many other planned landscapes [at Woodlawn] have completely disappeared."

One could expect a show of wealth by these titans of industry and business, some robber barons, who made up not only the wealthiest people in New York but the wealthiest people in America, by far. But most of the men in these families died first. The plans, execution, and upkeep of these eternal estates were mostly handled by women: their widows and daughters. The role of the widow or the heiress, at a time in society when most women had few rights, let alone a professional career, was a powerful one. These permanent female residents of Woodlawn were, for a time, the guardians of not only their husbands' legacies, but the legacy of their family as a whole.

Other female artists like Farrand found a place for their work at Woodlawn. Near the Harkness mausoleum is the resting place of Vernon and Irene Castle, an early twentieth-century dancing duo and the stars of several silent films. Vernon enlisted in World War I and was determined to fight as a pilot. Tragically, he perished in a crash during a training exercise in Fort Worth, Texas, in 1918.

Irene had seen the work of sculptor Sally James Farnham at the National Academy of Design, and asked her to expand upon a work for Vernon's grave at Woodlawn. The result is a gorgeous sculpture known lovingly as "the exhausted dancer" within the cemetery. Cast in bronze, the nude figure of a woman sits atop a pedestal, arms and head thrown down in either exhaustion or grief, or both. But its installation at Woodlawn was controversial due to its "expressive nudity." After a review by cemetery administrators, the dancer was approved. Though Irene would marry three more times, when she died in 1969, she was laid to rest next to Vernon under Farnham's sculpture at Woodlawn. "Every time I visit the grave," she once wrote in a letter to Woodlawn, "I feel impatient to get there."

Like Farrand, Farnham came from a wealthy family and traveled extensively in Europe as a young woman. Though she was mostly self-educated and self-trained, as art school wasn't open to

women during the early 1900s, Farnham went on to create several memorials at Woodlawn and had major commissions of public sculpture, like her statue of Simon Bolivar in Central Park.

To plan a walk through Woodlawn that feels as spontaneous as one in a rural park cemetery might not be possible due to its "segmented" lawn plan. Instead, it helps to think of Woodlawn as an outdoor museum. The practice of memorial art at this level is just not done anymore. Woodlawn's landscape lawn plan was a step in the direction of the modern cemetery, to the "memorial park" structure, which exhibits no raised tombstones, much less elaborate personal monuments. As the costs of mausolea and other funerary art grew, and cremation rose in popularity, cemeteries became more regimented and frugal. The architecture and art at Woodlawn represent a vibrant era of memorial artwork that isn't possible to see anywhere else.

This art includes Tiffany stained glass. At one point, Tiffany Studios had an entire Memorial Windows department, and the fruits of that labor, often a collaboration between the mausoleum owner and the studio, are featured in many mausoleums at Woodlawn. Other than the Metropolitan Museum, Woodlawn has the largest collection of Tiffany stained glass in the world. It can be found in the Harbeck, Fahnestock, Colby, Wyckoff, Cohan, and Miller mausoleums. The whole of the Currier mausoleum, including its interior, structure, and landscape, was designed by Tiffany Studios.

Other than Tiffany, America's finest stained-glass artist was a woman named Helen Maitland Armstrong. Armstrong trained with her father, Maitland Armstrong, and, more formally, with the Art Students League of New York. Like Beatrix Farrand and Sally James Farnham, Armstrong had the benefit of a European education. Her father was also a diplomat and she was born in Florence, Italy. Eventually, her father made her a partner in their design firm, and Armstrong went on to create dozens of windows for private clients—remember, women were mostly barred from public commissions. Some of Armstrong's finest work includes her sixteen windows for Alva Belmont's memorial chapel at Woodlawn.

Woodlawn does open these mausoleums to the public occasionally for themed tours and for one popular tour called the Illuminated Mausoleum Tour, in which the largest mausoleums are opened and illuminated in color at evening. But on a typical day, these incredible works of art are not open to the public. Woodlawn doesn't have the kind of security and labor to facilitate the mausoleums being open for visitors to walk through on a daily basis. At the end of the day, Woodlawn is a cemetery, and these mausoleums, fine as they are, are still private graves.

Even those monuments that seem impenetrable to the elements, like the Foster mausoleum, are difficult to maintain. Its sheer size, rising on a hill just a short walk down Central Avenue, is enough to knock you off your feet. Though it has no walls, it is technically, by design standards, a mausoleum. It most closely resembles a gigantic Greek or Roman canopy tomb. The man who designed it for himself was named William F. Foster, and he made a fortune with his patent of fasteners for gloves. He died in 1895.

By 1931, the monument was in total disrepair. Desperate, the cemetery put out feelers for heirs. In a letter to one of the family's lawyers, Woodlawn wrote, "In time to come should it be dangerous or so badly in need of repairs that it would become unsightly, the cemetery would have the right to take it down and inter the bodies in the lot." *Quelle horreur.*

The husband of one of the heirs eventually responded that the family didn't really have the funds to execute the repairs that the cemetery required. "Four of the five are women whose income by reason of the depression has suffered considerably," he wrote. It seems rather unbelievable that the monument, given its stature and appearance today, could have ever been in such terrible shape. But there is a reason Americans eventually abandoned these elaborate and oftentimes ostentatious monuments—they are expensive to maintain. Families move. People die.

Woodlawn's popularity with the wealthy undoubtedly came from its proximity to Manhattan and the space that was available for those with high hopes for an imposing monument. To build a mausoleum like the Belmont or the Harbeck, you need a big lot. Green-Wood didn't really have the space, and so the uber-rich went to Woodlawn, outdoing each other with these "mini-estates."

Once the area around Central Avenue had been filled with these little mansions, though, a different kind of artist came to

Woodlawn. Thanks perhaps to the cemetery's proximity to Harlem and the artists of the Harlem Renaissance, Duke Ellington planned his eternal resting place at Woodlawn. He was such a planner that upon purchasing his plot he had his parents moved there. When he died in 1974, it was a huge loss to the jazz community. Twelve thousand people attended his funeral at the Cathedral of St. John the Divine. In subsequent years, a number of musicians of all stripes but especially those in the world of jazz have become

permanent residents of Woodlawn, all to be close to Duke. This section of the cemetery has come to be known as "jazz heaven."

Locating Duke is no easy task. It's quite a walk from the main entrance. I don't know what I was expecting, but his stone is not even raised; it lies flat in the ground, making it very tricky to spot, nestled in an island between two pathways, under a few trees. What is not difficult to see, however, is Miles Davis's gigantic tombstone, the size of a small boat, which is just to the right on the other side of the drive from Ellington. Sir Miles's tombstone is emblazoned with an illustration of his trumpet and the first two measures of the 1954 tune "Solar," from his album *Walkin'*. Just next to Miles, up the side of the hill, is drummer Max Roach.

Singer Celia Cruz, saxophonist Coleman Hawkins, bandleader King Oliver, and trumpeter Cootie Williams are just a few of the legends laid to rest near their beloved Duke.

When I finally found Ellington and his family, I stepped aside to take a few photos. It is difficult to comprehend the far-reaching influence of one man on modern music. More than two thousand works have been attributed to Duke Ellington since his death. I instinctively looked to the area on the other side of the sidewalk and noticed a beautiful, plain granite tombstone dotted with bright red tulips. Severely lacking in my knowledge of jazz, I loved the epitaph: "Flying home." Upon a quick Google search, it was revealed to be the resting place of Lionel Hampton, "King of the Vibes," whose signature song was, yes, "Flying Home."

Before jazz heaven, though, most people making a pilgrimage to Woodlawn did so in search of its most famous permanent resident, Herman Melville. When Melville died in 1891, he was not a literary success. In the last twenty years of his life, he had weathered a series of failures and his finances were tight. His family described his behavior as erratic, and friends pointed out his moodiness, anxiety, exhaustion, and heavy drinking. He left *Billy Budd* unfinished, and the book wasn't even discovered until 1919, published in 1924. It seems unbelievable, but *Moby-Dick* had been out of print for the last four years of Melville's life. Writing to his friend Nathaniel Hawthorne after the publication of his novel *Pierre*, Melville lamented his fate: "Though I wrote the Gospels in this century, I should die in the gutter."

Melville most likely ended up at Woodlawn because it was close to home. His two sons preceded him in death. Malcolm died of a self-inflicted gunshot wound at the age of eighteen, and Stanwix was found dead in a San Francisco hotel room at the age of thirty-six, most likely from tuberculosis. Herman's wife, Elizabeth, joined him in death in 1906, his daughter Elizabeth in 1908. His youngest child, Frances, is buried at Mount Auburn Cemetery in Cambridge, Massachusetts.

The rest of the Melvilles are buried in an unassuming plot in the center of the Catalpa section of the cemetery, surrounded by strangers. Nearby is the writer E. L. Doctorow, who perhaps, like the musicians in jazz heaven with Duke Ellington, wanted to be close to Melville. Melville's small gravestone is adorned with a scroll.

In death Melville has become one of America's most beloved writers. He was a New Yorker through and through. Born to an affluent family in New York City, he spent five years at sea, lived in Massachusetts for a time (where he befriended Nathaniel Hawthorne), and then returned home to New York, where he died at age seventy-two.

His wayward spirit is described in the first pages of *Moby-Dick*, attributed to Ishmael: "Whenever I find myself growing grim about the mouth; whenever it is a damp, drizzly November in my soul; whenever I find myself involuntarily pausing before coffin warehouses, and bringing up the rear of every funeral I meet; and especially whenever my hypos get such an upper hand of me, that

it requires a strong moral principle to prevent me from deliberately stepping into the street, and methodically knocking people's hats off—then, I account it high time to get to sea as soon as I can."

I sometimes feel about cemeteries the way Melville felt about the sea.

Another writer at Woodlawn is the opposite of Melville: incredibly famous in life and shamefully forgotten in death, Nellie Bly is located clear across the cemetery, what feels like miles from Melville. For decades she rested at Woodlawn in an unmarked grave.

In the late 1880s, Bly (the pen name of Elizabeth Cochran Seaman) became one of the most famous writers in the United States, pioneering a kind of writing that today we'd recognize as investigative journalism. She went into the Women's Lunatic Asylum on Blackwell Island undercover in order to write about the horrific conditions of most mental institutions at that time. The resulting exposé, *Ten Days in a Mad-House*, had enormous repercussions on the medical community.

Coming off the success of the asylum story, Nellie pitched the idea to her editor for her to undertake a real-life *Around the World in Eighty Days*. She completed her travels in seventy-two days, traveling alone, becoming a national sensation. Despite her enormous success in the field of journalism, Nellie married a wealthy older man, the manufacturer Robert Seaman, and because of his poor health dedicated the remainder of her working days to his company. After he died, a series of financial problems plagued Nellie, and she died of pneumonia, broke and alone, at the age of fifty-seven in 1922.

In 1978, the New York Press Club erected a tombstone over what is believed to be the general area of Nellie's final resting place. Her epitaph reads, "A Famous News Reporter."

As the Bronx experienced a boom in immigration after World War I, Woodlawn's neighborhoods also came to reflect the immigrant experience in New York City. Entire sections are filled with Italian, German, and, most recently, Latinx communities who have built their own permanent homes at Woodlawn, reflecting the change in the populace of the borough. The showy mausoleums at the front of the cemetery meant that successful immigrants wanted to be buried at Woodlawn when their time came. Immigrants like the Straus family, co-owners of Macy's department store.

Isidor Straus was born in Germany and immigrated to the United States in 1852. After building a successful crockery business with his father, which he then sold to Macy's, he and his brother became partners in the department store. After serving as a congressman for two years, Isidor enjoyed his retirement. He and his wife, Ida, were returning from a European vacation when their ship struck an iceberg in the middle of the Atlantic Ocean. Though women and children were given priority on the lifeboats, Ida refused to leave her husband's side. According to witnesses, she said something like, "As we have lived, so we will die, together." Isidor and Ida both went down with the *Titanic* that night, April 14, 1912.

The six children of Isidor and Ida planned the memorial for their parents at Woodlawn, designed by James Gamble Rogers, architect of the Harkness mausoleum. It features a structure of three separate mausoleums, one for each of their three sons' families, and its central feature is an Egyptian funeral barge under

which Isidor is buried. Ida's remains were never recovered. On the inward side of the barge is her epitaph, which reads, "Lost at sea."

Immigrants also found success as artists and sculptors at Woodlawn. The Piccirilli brothers were a family (father and six sons) of Italian stone carvers who came from Massa Carrara in Tuscany and settled in the Bronx. Outside of Woodlawn, some of their most famous works are the USS *Maine* National Monument in Central Park and the lions that guard the New York Public Library. One of their most moving works of art at Woodlawn is a memorial for New York City's beloved mayor Fiorello La Guardia.

La Guardia, the son of an Italian father and Jewish mother from Trieste, was friends with Attilio Piccirilli, and the sculptor gave La Guardia a bronze statue of a child called *The First Step* in celebration of his wedding. After La Guardia's first wife, Thea, and their baby, Fioretta, tragically died within a few months of each other in 1921, Attilio created a beautiful memorial for the lost mother and child. In their shared tombstone, Thea appears in a field, flowers resting on her lap, arms outstretched as her daughter waddles over to her. At the top left-hand corner their epitaph reads simply, "Thea and Fioretta Fiorello."

Though the Piccirilli brothers were responsible for some of the most renowned works of public sculpture in the United States, by the 1930s the family inexplicably closed their business without archiving any of their design records. Woodlawn's archive at the Avery Library contains the only surviving records of the Piccirilli brothers' enormous contribution to American art.

By 1930 the Bronx had been crippled by bootlegging and other criminal activity, leading to a mass exodus of its affluent, mostly white residents. With the rise of affordable housing in the way of housing projects, lower-income groups, at that time mostly African American and Hispanic people, came to call the Bronx home, a trend that continues to the present day. Robert Moses's Cross Bronx

Expressway, begun in 1948 and completed in 1972, only exacerbated an already precarious housing situation for Bronx residents. As Robert Caro has written in his expansive biography of Moses, *The Power Broker*, Moses had little regard for the people living in the way of his freeway. Thousands of Bronx residents were left homeless or barely surviving in makeshift slums without sufficient shelter or even running water. Architect Ronald Shiffman wrote that Moses's Cross Bronx Expressway essentially "ripped through the heart of the Bronx." In some ways, the borough has never recovered.

What's ironic is that Moses himself, who died in 1981, is entombed at Woodlawn, in a community mausoleum, the apartment version of burial, on the Jerome Avenue side of the cemetery—the very Jerome Avenue that was so destroyed by his expressway.

It's no surprise that in the complaints folder for Woodlawn the majority of the serious issues about the upkeep of the cemetery do not begin to mount until the late 1970s. Every cemetery has complaints—with a myriad of lot holders and families there are bound to be complaints over the years. But Woodlawn, like Green-Wood, and in fact any other large cemetery in the United States, had, like the Bronx, begun its sharp decline in the 1970s—a decline and neglect that would last well into the 1990s.

One letter in the Woodlawn complaints folder held in Columbia's Avery Library is from a woman who tried to gain access to her father's grave at Woodlawn one afternoon at 4:30 p.m. She was barred entry because the security guard said that the cemetery would be closing in a few minutes and that he didn't get paid past closing hours to stand around and wait. It is a heartbreaking letter, in which she describes to the cemetery superintendent that Woodlawn looks more like a "junkyard" than a cemetery. It was written in 1981. Other similar letters describe the graves being "in a sorry and sad state" in 1977, "a positive disgrace" in 1978, and even in 1996, "what a shame, what a mess." In another complaint lodged in 1996, the writer says that the graves are in "neglect and filth."

Cemeteries, like the neighborhoods of the Bronx or other disenfranchised parts of Brooklyn, even Manhattan, were pushed to the wayside, out of sight, out of mind. With advances in medicine, by the 1970s death had become hospitalized in the sense that most Americans died in hospitals, which is still the case today. The lack of interaction with the deceased, before death in the hospital and afterward as the body was handed over to the funeral home, contributes to a denial of death that has typified most Americans' experience since then. The popularity of cremation (most Americans choose this option—66 percent on average, though it varies from state to state) was the stake in the heart of American cemeteries. If the majority of people choose cremation and most of the survivors take the cremains with them, the cemetery's role in society is ever dwindling. Today, for most, driving by a cemetery is nothing more than an unwelcome reminder that life ends.

Woodlawn's home, in the Bronx, is a fitting one. Both the borough and the cemetery began as enclaves of the wealthy in New York, and both have gone through a dark period of neglect. Like any other kind of social service—a church, a library, a synagogue, schools—these things are kept strong through the support of the people who live there. But if the people who belong to the community are disenfranchised, it becomes more and more difficult to maintain places like cemeteries. A floundering community must focus on the elements of society that are more essential to them on a daily basis rather than preserving a history or heritage. But the neglect of cemeteries directly contributes to an erosion of Americans' relationship with the past, and with their future. Luckily there is hope. As the Bronx goes through a revitalization thanks to help from city officials and developers and its residents, so too does Woodlawn, getting a boost from being named in the National Register of Historic Places in 2011.

There is hope that visitors to Woodlawn will now be able to experience its magic with its gates thrown open. Thanks to help from the National Register and to countless volunteers who work to keep Woodlawn's treasures in good shape, the cemetery has recaptured its original sheen. And it is still very much an active cemetery. In 2017, Woodlawn made $8 million in sales. There are still twenty-five acres available for those interested in becoming a permanent part of its vibrant history.

Melville wrote in *Moby-Dick*, "Heaven have mercy on us all—Presbyterians and Pagans alike—for we are all somehow dreadfully cracked about the head, and sadly need mending." Americans have dealt with the inevitable for decades by not dealing with it. We're all "dreadfully cracked" and most of us never pause to question why. It's inevitable that burial rituals and methods will change as technology changes. But the erasure of cemeteries from national consciousness is an erasure of American history. How does one begin to navigate the future without a solid knowledge of the past?

In 1913, a woman named Anna Bliss held a design competition for the right to design the memorial for her stepdaughter, who had died after a fall. A sculptor named Robert L. Aitken rose to the challenge and the Piccirilli brothers realized what remains one of Woodlawn's most beloved monuments.

The effect of the Anna Bliss plot is cinematic. Walking down Myosotis Avenue, my eye was drawn to the Straus memorial, which is on the same level as the street. But as I turned to the right in search of the Bliss memorial, it appeared at the top of a hill so expansive and so green, it looked like a movie set. The monument features two figures, one male and one female, who represent Hope and Faith, walking toward something with conviction. Behind them is a long, curved white bench that stretches across the entire lawn and bears a quotation from Wordsworth: "Our souls have sight of that immortal sea which brought us hither."

Visitors to Woodlawn have long been moved by the sculpture and wanted to know more about the woman who commissioned it. "A few weeks ago I had the privilege to visit the beautiful Woodlawn Cemetery," Minnie E. Allen wrote to the cemetery in

1953. "I was deeply impressed by many fine works of art. Among them is the Bliss Memorial which gave me the greatest joy. Is there a picture of it? What is the history behind this monument? What can you tell me about the artist?"

Another visitor, Mrs. Joseph Mitchell, in 1937 wrote asking for more information. "Could you give me some information about the beautiful memorial known as the Bliss memorial? I had some visitors from out of town who were interested. I promised

to let them know what I could find out." Woodlawn's superintendent at the time responded, "Mrs. Bliss, during her lifetime, had very definite ideas as to the type of Memorial she wished and we understand that this one was the outcome of a competition among Sculptors, the result being the beautiful work by Robert L. Aitken."

The way the sunlight fell on the stone fabric of the female figure's dress when I stood there that summer afternoon gave the monument an animated effect, as if the couple was living, moving. The Anna Bliss memorial is a reflection of Woodlawn, and of the spirit of the Bronx itself—constantly changing, steadfastly hopeful, always in forward motion.

SILVER CORD

EVERGREENS CEMETERY,
BROOKLYN

In 1905, a visitor was wandering the grounds of Evergreens Cemetery in Brooklyn when he noticed the door to one mausoleum was ajar. He poked his head in and found an elderly gentleman on the floor of the tomb in distress. After reaching a policeman who was on duty in the cemetery that day, the two managed to convey the man, who had suffered a stroke, to the nearby hospital. He died several months later.

As it turned out, the man was well known to Evergreens Cemetery, and the mausoleum he had been discovered in was the resting place of his wife. By the time Jonathan was discovered on the floor of the mausoleum, his wife, Mary, had been dead for twelve years.

Upon her death in 1893 Mary was first entombed in her family mausoleum at Evergreens, which belonged to her mother and father. Jonathan would visit frequently—a little too frequently for the taste of Mary's father. Luckily for the grieving husband, Mary's father died, allowing Jonathan to visit her as often as he liked. But even with that freedom, Jonathan craved more privacy.

He moved Mary to a different mausoleum, one he had built with the inscription "Jonathan and Mary E. Reed." He placed another empty casket next to hers, preparing to join her in their new home. Every day, he would walk from his house on Marcy Avenue and South Ninth Street to be at Evergreens when the gates opened at 6:00 a.m. He would remain in the mausoleum with his departed wife until he was forced to leave at 6:00 p.m., when the cemetery closed to visitors.

But spending the whole day with Mary in the mausoleum was not enough for Jonathan Reed. He believed that his wife was still alive, but that the warmth had simply left her body. He installed an oilstove to heat the mausoleum and brought in mementos from their life together, including Mary's unfinished knitting, several paintings she had done, and even their pet parrot, who, upon his death, was stuffed and placed alongside Mary in the crypt.

Friends came to visit, trying to persuade the widower that his wife was dead and that he needed to move on with his life outside the cemetery. But the old man would not listen. He became something of a celebrity. According to the *New York Times*, nearly seven thousand people came to tour the cemetery in hopes of catching a glimpse of him. The paper reported that he would carry on long conversations with his deceased wife, never believing she was gone.

The years passed, nearly a decade, until the stranger noticed the unhinged door that afternoon.

Following Jonathan's death, friends and family discovered that he had hung several portraits of Mary that chronicled her life, from childhood to just before her death. Another painting, hung

on the walls of the mausoleum and created by a "well-known artist," according to the *Times*, was entitled *Crossing the Styx*.

After ten years of living in his wife's tomb, Jonathan Reed had
finally done just that—crossed the River Styx. He was placed in the
matching metallic casket he had chosen for himself and joined Mary
in their shared home. The doors to the mausoleum were sealed.

Established in 1849, Evergreens, located a short walk from
the Bushwick Avenue–Aberdeen Street stop on the L train, is
one of the many cemeteries that popped up in the surrounding
boroughs of New York City following the passage of the Rural
Cemetery Act in 1847. It is quite large at 225 acres and over
526,000 interments. Notable historical monuments include a
memorial to the victims of the Triangle Shirtwaist Factory fire in
1911. The six who perished in the fire were buried here unidenti-
fied. Historian Michael Hirsch was able to make a positive identi-
fication one hundred years later, in 2011.

Evergreens is also the resting place for a great number of
actors, mostly vaudevillians, and several famous black entertainers,

including tap dancer Bill "Bojangles" Robinson, pianist Thomas "Blind Tom" Wiggins, and jazz singer Adelaide Hall. Robinson's epitaph reads, "Danced his way into the hearts of millions."

At one time, Evergreens was a very popular and extremely busy cemetery. In 1929, there were 4,673 burials. Today, it is positively serene and disarmingly quiet.

The mausoleum of Jonathan and Mary Reed remains sealed today. It is nestled in a lane of a few other mausoleums at Evergreens, modestly resting from the gaze of visitors who know nothing of its macabre love story.

I first traveled to Evergreens specifically to see the mausoleum of Mary Reed for a story I was writing on the place. But once I arrived I was delighted to discover that the cemetery itself is a hidden jewel. Just a short ride on the train from my home, it was the closest thing I had in New York to a neighborhood cemetery. Like other park cemeteries, it contains beautiful funerary art and fantastic stories, like that of Mary and Jonathan, but it's more demure than Green-Wood or Woodlawn. Evergreens is the quiet friend at the party, standing just apart from the crowd.

In the final days of my pregnancy, I couldn't venture very far. But just a few days before I went into labor I made it to Evergreens. It was a blissfully cool morning in the midst of late summer humidity. There was no one else in the cemetery that day. I walked the grounds deeply contemplative about the new chapter in my life barreling toward me.

Cemeteries are wonderful places to take a walk and to clear your head. It's interesting, too, to see what jumps out at me or what memorials I notice depending on the day and what's on my mind.

I saw a small silver gate in a section just off the path. These were known as rail lots. Not many of their gates survive, as the government used them for scrap metal during World Wars I and II. This one once marked the entrance to a section called Silver Cord. The gate rested on the stones, looking woefully out of place.

The silver cord is most frequently alluded to as the energy that connects a soul to its physical body. In astral projection, or in out-of-body experiences, people have claimed to have seen a silver cord running from their bodies into space. It reminds me of the phrase "cellar door," which, from a phonaesthetics standpoint, is supposedly the most beautiful phrase in the English language.

I thought of the silver cord that had kept Jonathan coming back to Mary, despite all obstacles, even death. We crave that connection to our loved ones, and when it's severed, it can be simply too painful to imagine that there's nothing that keeps us tethered. Jonathan Reed continued to live his life as if nothing had changed, as if his physical presence would somehow prevent his wife from being gone.

The connotations of "silver cord" for me, nine months pregnant, were fairly obvious. But its origins come from a passage in the Bible, Ecclesiastes 12:6-7: "Remember him—before the silver cord is severed, or the golden bowl is broken; before the pitcher is shattered at the spring, or the wheel broken at the well, and the dust returns to the ground it came from, and the spirit returns to God who gave it."

CITIZENS

CALVARY CEMETERY
AND
MOUNT ZION CEMETERY,
QUEENS

Twin cities of the living and the dead greet visitors to New York City in a devastating tableau.

The second city, a mirror image of the skyline of Manhattan, is Calvary Cemetery, in Queens, New York.

Currently, 2.3 million people live in the borough of Queens. There are three million people buried in Calvary Cemetery.

The fact that the dead outnumber the living here is a difficult concept to get one's mind around. Calvary is one of the only cemeteries that is just as impressive standing inside as it is outside looking in. The sheer size of the cemetery gives it an air of impenetrability. The thousands upon thousands of stones have a dizzying effect on the viewer.

The best thing to do when one is intimidated is to jump right in. And so, much to the surprise of the millions who are at rest at Calvary, I'm coming to pay a visit.

Though it was consecrated in 1848, there are graves inside Calvary that date back to the early 1700s. When the Trustees of St. Patrick's Cathedral wanted to acquire the land, they had to purchase it from the Alsop family, who had a farm here and had used a section of it as their family burying ground from 1718 to 1889. They did sell, under the instructions that the family would always have access to their thirty gravestones.

Why did a Manhattan Roman Catholic church buy in Queens? In 1847, New York City passed a law that no more burials should take place on the island of Manhattan. The Rural Cemetery Act spurred on the creation of many of New York's largest and most beautiful cemeteries: Green-Wood, Woodlawn, Calvary, and more. Now with 365 acres, Calvary Cemetery is the largest cemetery in the United States in terms of the number of people buried there.

In this book I have tried to impart a story about New York, what each cemetery says about New York. The story at Calvary is the story of New York, in every sense of the word because it is the story of immigrants.

One particular tombstone in Calvary is reflective of the cemetery itself, covered in dozens, even hundreds, of names. The Mahony family chronicles generation upon generation who came to New York, lived here, and died here. So many of the obelisks in First Calvary, the oldest part of the cemetery, are Irish names. And not only Irish names but Irish birthplaces: "Born in Cork." "Born in Killarney." "Born in Galway." Over 90 percent of the tombstones in Calvary list a place of birth.

One Irishman's tombstone reads like a microbiography: "Richard Byrnes, native of County Cavan, Ireland, Colonel, 28th Mass. Vol. Infantry, 1st Lieutenant, 5th U.S. Calvary, Sergeant Major, 1st U.S. Calvary, 1st Sergeant, 1st U.S. Dragoons. Mortally wounded leading the famed Irish brigade in battle at Cold Harbor,

Virginia, June 3, 1864. Died at age of 31 years, June 12, 1864. His devoted wife Ellen, died January 12, 1911. Loving daughters Margaret 1862–1900 and Catherine 1863–1913. 'Put your trust and confidence in God. Ask His blessing. Kiss my poor little children for me. I fear nothing, thank Heaven, but my sins. Do not let your spirits sink; we will meet again.' —Richard."

The Great Famine in Ireland began in 1845, sending thousands of Irish people across the ocean as their only hope of survival. One million people died and another million fled. Ireland, in terms of its population, has never fully recovered. By 1850, the Irish made up 25 percent of the population of New York City.

Annie Moore, the first person to be processed through Ellis Island, is buried here. She was just seventeen, traveling from Ireland with her two younger brothers to meet her parents, who had already settled in New York. The three siblings spent Christmas at sea and arrived for the unveiling of the new immigration center. Upon entry she was given a ten-dollar gold piece by agents. She eventually married and had eleven children, only five of whom survived to become adults. Rumor has it that Annie was such a large woman that when she died of congestive heart failure her casket had to be removed from her apartment by crane.

Nearly equal to the Irish population of Calvary is the Italian population. In the early 1900s, nearly two million Italian people immigrated to New York. By 1930, Italians made up 17 percent of the population. As Catholics, the Irish and Italian dead at Calvary are marked by a cross. The cemetery name itself references Mount Calvary, where Jesus was crucified.

And every stone tells a story, like that of Larry Carella, buried with his parents, "Killed in action in Korea," just twenty-three years old.

The holy family greets you in stunning displays of granite and stone. One of my favorite family plots is that of the Iervolino family, which depicts the pietà, the Virgin Mary with surrounding female figures attending to the broken body of Jesus Christ.

Likenesses of the family patriarch, Luigi, and matriarch, Angela Rosa, adorn the family stone.

The Iervolino plot is located just in the right spot of the cemetery so that no matter what time of day it is, it's always enveloped in a soft glow. Above the two men holding the body of Jesus is the Virgin, arms extended in grief. Above her left shoulder is a younger woman, who clings to her in a way that seems to communicate both the need and the offer of comfort.

I am not a religious person, but some of the religious artwork at Calvary gives me pause.

On my way down the hill near the Italian section, I noticed a rather charming statue of Jesus holding a lamb as the shepherd attends to his flock. Someone had placed a small bouquet of red and white fake flowers at his crook. I wondered who could have such a nice monument all to themselves, then quickly realized this was not the resting place of one but of many Roman Catholic priests.

Their stones, all uniform, flank the statue of Jesus as shepherd in neat rows that stretch on and on through the yard. Upon review,

each stone not only lists each priest's dates, but also the date on which he had been ordained, with the epitaph "Rest in Peace, o Priest of Jesus Christ."

Just across the street from the priests' burying ground is Calvary's chapel, designed by Raymond F. Almirall. It was originally intended as a mortuary chapel specifically reserved for priests, which probably accounts for their proximity. Still an active chapel, once a week it hosts a funeral mass for all of those buried within Calvary.

A short walk down the winding drive in front of the chapel, there are a few freestanding mausoleums. The one for the Stevely family bears a quotation from *Romeo and Juliet*, but rather than the typical romantic association, it is a mournful declaration from daughter to mother: "Mother darling, parting is such sweet sorrow that I'll say goodnight until the morrow, your daughter."

Another mausoleum bears a small epitaph inscribed on its side, near the bottom left-hand corner for a baby boy, not yet two. "David Ennis McQuail, April 24, 1953–July 4, 1954."

Aside from the administrative building, the chapel, and a few freestanding mausoleums, Calvary is mostly made up of single or family plots. But there is one gigantic mausoleum located in a mausoleum row of sorts at the top of the hill. The Johnston brothers owned a successful fabric store that specialized in silks. The two were so flush with cash that they built this gargantuan mausoleum at Calvary for nearly $100,000, a huge sum in the 1800s. Though there are thirty crypts, only six are occupied. The brothers squandered their fortunes, and the last surviving brother died ill and insane in a barn.

What's that Bible verse about a rich man and the eye of a needle?

Though the mausoleum still stands at the top of the hill with a nice view of the lower part of First Calvary, it's a beautiful ruin. The brass door is cracked and the stone carvings are weathered, barely visible from pollution and age. Christ, bearing the cross, peers over the top of the domed mausoleum, while a serious angel applies to the heavens.

As one of the tombstones near the Johnston mausoleum implores, "Say One Hail Mary."

I had long been acquainted with Calvary as the country's largest cemetery. But I wanted to make sure I had covered my ground with another group of immigrants, a defining group of citizens who have come to have an enormous influence on New York: the Jews.

Just a short but perilous drive from Calvary is Mount Zion Cemetery, one of the country's largest Jewish cemeteries. Established in 1893, Mount Zion has nearly the same number of interments as Green-Wood but is a third its size, meaning the people buried here are packed in like sardines.

The reason for this is two-fold. First, the prevalence of burial societies in turn-of-the-century Jewish cemeteries in New York created group burial. If you belonged to a burial society, or a professional group that had a burial plot, it was considerably cheaper to be buried. But that meant that the society itself had the freedom to squeeze as many members into one section as possible. Second, Jewish tradition states that only one person may be placed in one grave, so unlike non-Jewish mausoleums or family crypts where you might have as many as ten or twenty people stacked on top of each other, Jewish graves must stand alone, albeit alongside one another.

My first visit to Mount Zion was an incredibly blustery gray but uncomfortably humid day. It matched my mood. I was

frustrated by the fact that I'd had to drive and was worried about what the situation with driving and parking would be once I got into the cemetery. Maspeth, Queens, where Mount Zion is situated, is heavily industrial. All the low-lying level factory buildings are covered in pollution and the streets are clogged with loud, gigantic trucks. Once I was off the freeway I found myself in gridlock waiting for an oil truck to make a three-point turn. Where was this cemetery?

Once there was a large gate that marked its entrance. Now, there is practically nothing that announces Mount Zion except for a humble sign. I pulled into the cemetery just as a landscaping truck was taking off from the administrative offices. Two men jumped into the bed of the truck as it pulled in front of me. I looked from side to side; there was nowhere to turn. It was an incredibly narrow single-lane road, with nothing but tombstones on both sides of us. I followed the truck for what seemed like hours as it dropped off its laborers in different sections. Finally, at the back of the cemetery it turned around, and I did the same, eventually parking next to it in a circular drive where there was more space.

One of the maintenance workers approached. "Is it okay if I park here?" I asked.

"Of course," he said quietly, "as long as cars get by. Are you looking for someone?"

In a new cemetery I always find it's better to have an answer to this question, lest I make the staff nervous.

"Yes, Nathanael West," I replied. "I think he's in this section over here."

The worker obligingly led me over to the section though he said he wasn't sure of the location. After a few minutes of walking down a small footpath, I found him: Nathanael West, the author of *Miss Lonelyhearts* and *The Day of the Locust*. West was a great writer but apparently not a very good driver. Returning from a hunting trip with his wife, Eileen (the inspiration for the play and later film *My Sister Eileen*), in Mexico, West ran a stop sign in El Centro, California, and both he and his wife were killed.

West's parents were Jewish Russian immigrants who lived on the Upper West Side of Manhattan, so when he and Eileen died, they joined his family at Mount Zion. His epitaph, on the top of the stone, reads, "Son." Underneath his name it says, almost apologetically, "Husband of Eileen."

"I found him!" I exclaimed to the group of workers laboring over an open grave.

"Is he a relation?" the man I'd spoken to asked.

"No, he was a famous writer."

There was an awkward pause as I stopped to take a few photos.

"How long have you worked here?" I said to the man.

"Oh, not long, five years maybe."

"Do you get many burials out here?"

"A year?"

"Yeah, in a year, how many?"

"Oh," he said, shaking his head. "Not many. One. Maybe two."

I walked back to where my car was parked and looked at the section adjacent to Nathanael West. In the center of the cemetery, there are two gigantic but inactive smokestacks. These belong to the incinerator of the now defunct New York Sanitation Department. Their presence gave a dystopian vibe to the whole place. The menacing gray sky only added to the effect.

"Thanks for your help," I told the nice man as I ventured into the section.

Like Calvary, Mount Zion was founded after the passage of the Rural Cemetery Act, which accounts for its overcrowding. The land upon which it was built was once swampland. This gives Mount Zion rich soil and beautiful and unexpected patches of lush greenery, like ferns, even daisies, amidst the claustrophobic tombstones and disconcerting industrial surroundings.

One of my favorite things about Mount Zion is its portraits. From the 1930s through the 1950s, a process called enameling allowed for portraits of the deceased to be burned into enamel plates and then placed onto the tombstones. There are so many gorgeous examples of enamel portraits at Mount Zion. Some are still in wonderful shape. Others, less so.

Rose Brauer, "beloved wife and dear mother, died Nov. 6, 1927, age 34 years" in a beautiful dress smiles shyly back at me, her portrait in nearly pristine condition.

Bessie Perlman, "died September 8, 1934, age 31 years," gamely confronts the camera straight on. She looks like a great friend. Her epitaph reads simply, "Beloved daughter and sister."

As I walked down the small footpath from the drive, I noticed I was walking slightly uphill. Nearly every single stone seemed to say "Beloved mother" or "Beloved father." All were covered in Hebrew and the symbols of the Jewish faith. The lettering, the stonework, and the enameled portraits were forged in undeniable love and appreciation.

I could see the smokestacks getting closer in my sightline. Then, I found I could not catch my breath.

Mount Zion erupts and unfolds itself in a clearing that seems to stretch on for miles and miles. The endless number of stones

seems to reach as far as the new trade tower, barely visible in the distance in Manhattan.

Today, there are 1.5 million Jewish people who call the New York City metro area home. That's more than the Jewish populations of Chicago, Philadelphia, San Francisco, and Washington, DC, *combined*.

The Jewish population of New York City reached a peak in the years following World War II, when at one point two million Jews made up a quarter of the city's population. Now, Jewish people make up about 13 percent of the city.

Mount Zion was the busiest in the years between 1930 and 1945. It's not difficult to imagine what would have happened to those Jewish people, the majority of them who are buried here at Mount Zion, had they not been citizens of New York at that time.

It's simultaneously devastating and uplifting to see the permanent homes of all of these Jewish people in their adopted home of New York City. The hundreds of thousands, together, their stones leaning against each other like wearied travelers.

The Irish and Italian immigrants of Calvary Cemetery undoubtedly played a huge role in the literal and cultural development of modern New York. Yet today most Americans, like myself, identify less as Irish or Italian (I am, in fact, both) than they do as plainly American. Jewish immigrants and Jewish people are

different. One could argue that there is no other group of immigrants that has had a deeper influence on the lifeblood of New York City.

Emma Lazarus was a Jewish woman who was born in New York City in 1849 and went on to become an activist and a poet. Her poem "The New Colossus" is emblazoned on a plaque at

the feet of the Statue of Liberty. It reads, in part, "Give me your tired, your poor, your huddled masses yearning to breathe free, the wretched refuse of your teeming shore. Send these, the homeless, tempest-tost to me, I lift my lamp beside the golden door!"

Lazarus is not buried at Mount Zion, but her legacy as the author of the most potent message about liberty and immigration resounds throughout the cemetery.

In the last several years, there has been a disturbing resurgence of white supremacy, bigotry, and isolationism in this country. Jewish cemeteries in St. Louis, New Jersey, and New York were marred by incidences of cemetery vandalism in 2017 and 2018. The last time our country (and, in fact, the world) witnessed the vandalization of Jewish cemeteries was before and during the Holocaust.

The goal of this book is to point out the hidden histories of cemeteries and what they can teach us as people. To neglect, even actively neglect, cemeteries is one thing. But to purposefully destroy them, to attack them in a hateful act of vandalism, is more than just willful ignorance. We have a word for it: terrorism.

Back in Calvary Cemetery, there is an avenue of champion trees that were planted in memory of those who died on 9/11, including eleven people who are buried at Calvary. A nearby plaque reads, "May these trees grow to maturity giving hope and strength to all New Yorkers." This section of the cemetery, with rows upon rows of small tombstones reaching endlessly toward the isle of Manhattan, directly overlooks where the towers once stood.

Congressman Joseph Conway spoke at the unveiling service in 2002, which doubled as a memorial service, highlighting the service of first responders with words from Lincoln's Gettysburg Address: "The world will little note nor remember what we say here, but it can never forget what they did here. We here highly resolve that these dead shall not have died in vain, that this nation under God shall have a new birth of freedom, and that the government of the people, by the people, for the people, shall not perish from this earth."

To quote from the Gettysburg Address at a 9/11 memorial might seem strange, but I think I understand what Congressman Conway was hoping to achieve.

Enclosed by a little gate within the cemetery is Calvary Park, the only New York City park to be located inside a cemetery.

Directly in front of Calvary Park is a large monument dedicated to the Fighting 69th, an all-Irish regiment that fought for the Union during the Civil War, and the 165th regiment, an Irish regiment that fought in World Wars I and II. A list on each side of the tablet names all the battles of the 69th and the 165th.

There are twenty-one Catholic Civil War soldiers buried in Calvary Park, underneath an obelisk protected by four very distinguished statues. There is nearly an identical memorial at Battle Hill, in Green-Wood Cemetery. My favorite of the four men carries an ax over his shoulder. "To the memory of the brave men," the memorial plaque reads, "who gave their lives to preserve the union 1861–1865."

These soldiers were immigrants to this country.

To preserve the union—and what does that union represent? We have Lincoln's answer: "the government of the people, by the people, for the people."

What could be better proof of true citizenship than to die for your adopted country?

When France extended the Statue of Liberty as a gift to the United States in 1886, the country did so in acknowledgment and celebration of America's abolition of slavery. In original plans for Lady Liberty's design, she held a broken chain, symbolizing the freedom of the enslaved, two pieces in each hand. The designers

ultimately thought the optics too controversial, so they moved the broken shackle to a less visible place at her feet.

The broken chain is barely visible amidst her long robes, but a closer look reveals a partially hidden, equally important part of the statue's symbolism. She greets immigrants to New York, those "tempest-tost," with her torch, lighting the way to freedom. If you look carefully at the Statue of Liberty from behind, though, you'll see that she is not standing still in greeting. She is walking forward with one foot raised. Liberated, she lights the way for others as she breaks her own chains.

LOCALS ONLY

GREEN RIVER CEMETERY,
EAST HAMPTON

Just a short drive from Green River Cemetery in a small town called Springs within East Hampton, New York, is the Pollock-Krasner House and Study Center. The small house and adjacent studio were the home and workspace of painter Jackson Pollock and his wife, the artist Lee Krasner.

I took a charming but meandering tour of the museum last summer, bringing my fourteen-month-old son who was, needless to say, less than impressed with the barn studio that still bears Pollock's splatter paints. As the tour guide explained Pollock's work habits while we removed our shoes and replaced them with little footies, my son wailed with boredom, more interested in the grass outside on the lawn.

When asked why she and Pollock never had any children, according to the guide, Krasner replied, "I already have one—Jackson."

Pollock was a prolific alcoholic and philanderer. Krasner spent most of their marriage taking care of him and completing very little work. When he died in a car crash, drunk at the wheel with his mistress, Ruth Kligman, who survived, and her friend Edith Metzger, who did not, Krasner buried him under a gigantic boulder in Green River, just up the road.

The year was 1956. Until then Green River had been a small local cemetery, founded in 1902. The origin of the name Green River is puzzling even to those whose families have lived in the area for decades, as there's no river, green or otherwise, anywhere nearby.

But Pollock's presence put Green River on the map, so to speak. Over the years it has become a veritable Who's Who in the American modern art scene: Stuart Davis, Elaine de Kooning, Jimmy Ernst, John Ferren, Perle Fine, Lee Krasner, Abraham Rattner, Ad Reinhart, and Hannah Wilke have been buried here. Famous writers and poets like Frank O'Hara, Jean Stafford, and A. J. Liebling have also come to call Green River home for eternity.

Visitors frequently leave Coke bottles on Frank O'Hara's grave, in homage to his poem "Having a Coke with You."

Some of these notable artists were Pollock's neighbors and had a direct link to the town of Springs, living and working there intermittently or even full-time. But most of them didn't have that connection, and Green River's status as the cemetery of famous artists has frustrated the residents of Springs, who feel they have more of a right to be buried here than out-of-towners, no matter how prominent they might be.

The impulse to be buried next to greatness is nothing new. Early churchyards placed wealthy patrons in the church crypt itself. Next to that, a parishioner's best hope was to be as close to the church wall as possible. Napoleon has his generals (or at least their hearts) entombed in a circle around him at Les Invalides. Hugh Hefner bragged about purchasing the space next to Marilyn Monroe in the wall crypt at Westwood Memorial in Los Angeles and made good on his boast by being placed there upon his death in 2017.

In the 1960s dead artists flocked to Green River to be close to Pollock. Now, to be buried in Green River is to become a permanent part of the New York artistic elite.

With Pollock's boulder well in my line of sight, I set about the cemetery to find the other prominent New Yorkers I wanted to see, including writer Jean Stafford. I had just finished her novel *The Mountain Lion*, and I knew she was buried at Green River with her third husband, *New Yorker* writer A. J. Liebling. It took me some time, but I finally found them side by side under a large tree just across the path from Lee and Jackson.

Jean had a troubled personal life. Her first marriage was to poet Robert Lowell, who crashed his car with Jean as his passenger; she suffered horrible injuries to her head and face, the basis for her short story "The Interior Castle." Throughout her life she

suffered from depression and alcoholism, dying of pulmonary disease at the age of sixty-three. She is buried under a slate tombstone with her name, dates, and what appears to be a snowflake. Liebling's matching stone, just next to hers, bears a fleur-de-lis and the epitaph "Blessed—he could bless."

An editor of mine told me a story about Stafford and Liebling, together one time at the *New Yorker* offices. A young writer who had just been hired and come into contact with Stafford's work for the first time found himself in the elevator with Liebling. "I wish I could write like her," he said to Liebling. Liebling smiled and nodded. "I know," he said. "Me too."

For good measure I walked all the way to the back of the cemetery, which is bordered by a small fence. A group of attractive blue-gray stones caught my eye, the two in the front most considerably:

> *Robert Steel*
> *December 23, 1965–May 8, 1984*
> *Fare you well my honey*
> *Fare you well my only true one*
> *All the birds that were singing*
> *Are flown except you alone*

> *Courtney Steel*
> *December 22, 1968–October 19, 1986*
> *What though the radiance*
> *Which was once so bright*
> *Be now forever taken*
> *From my sight*

My mind hurried to make calculations. Robert and Courtney must have been brother and sister. Both died so young—Robert at eighteen and Courtney at seventeen, just two years later. A quick search turned up a horrific double tragedy for this family in so short a time. Robert died of bone cancer and Courtney in a hit-and-run in Manhattan.

Courtney was the student body president of Spence School at the time of her death. Though the family made no comment to the notice that ran in the *New York Times*, her neighbor, Louis Marx, said, "She was intelligent and of impeccable character—a lovely child of a lovely family."

Just adjacent to the Steels I noticed a tombstone that looked brand-new, its granite clean and white, and there were several roses strewn all around the plot. I walked up to get a closer look.

Jean Stein
1934–2017

The name sounded familiar. Jean Stein—once an editor at the *Paris Review*—had also been the coauthor, with George Plimpton, of a wonderful biography of Edie Sedgwick. The *Paris Review* is what had brought me to New York. I applied for and was granted

an internship with the literary magazine in the summer of 2006 after I graduated from college. A strange feeling of coincidence and déjà vu came over me standing at Jean's grave, thinking about my beginnings in New York.

Then I remembered: I had read it in the *New York Times*. Stein had died from suicide only recently. She leapt from her Manhattan penthouse apartment on May 2, 2017.

I was standing there September 17, 2018. There must have just been an unveiling ceremony, which is common in the Jewish religion. A person is usually buried promptly according to tradition, and the tombstone is not installed until a year later, even longer. When it is placed at the gravesite, family and friends attend what is known as its unveiling. This accounted for the fresh flowers. They looked like they had been left not hours before.

Stein went to Paris as a young student in 1955 intent on interviewing William Faulkner. She did—and reportedly had an affair with him. She later offered the interview to the *Paris Review* if they would make her an editor there in exchange. And so they did.

I walked around the back of Jean's stone on my way up the hill toward the entrance. I noticed there was an inscription on the back of the gravestone. It turns out Faulkner is the author of Stein's epitaph, the same words he used in dedicating *A Fable* to her: "For Jean, generous and thoughtful as you are. Never afraid as you should be. Happy and fortunate, as you deserve to be."

Stein is located in an area behind Pollock's boulder that looks like a new addition to the cemetery. And indeed it is. In 1987, the local man who owns the land behind Pollock sold one acre to the cemetery. But before the town could breathe a sigh of relief in acquiring more burial space, a woman named Courtney Sale Ross purchased basically all of the new plots. In 1992, Ross, the widow of Steven J. Ross, "who built a family funeral parlor business into Time Warner, Inc.," according to the *New York Times*, purchased 110 plots in the newly opened section of Green River Cemetery at a cost of $77,000.

Green River is an incredibly small, three-acre cemetery. As the *Times* has reported, it took eighty-five years for the first two acres to fill up. So when the cemetery had access to the land that made it a third larger than before, and nearly all the space was bought up by one single person, tempers flared.

"There is animosity," Deanna Tikkanen, once president of the Green River Cemetery Association, told the *Times*. "People with money are buying up the plots and they are not leaving anything for the local people."

The situation at Green River is illustrative of the plight of the Hamptons itself. Before the celebrities invaded, a group that reads like the guest list of the Vanity Fair Oscar Party, the Hamptons

was a working-class neighborhood. Now it's virtually impossible to even get to the area. One best have access to a helicopter to avoid the gridlock on the two-lane road. The cemeteries are no different. There are very few plots remaining in any of the Hamptons' graveyards. Thankfully, after the Ross debacle, Green River was able to purchase another acre and has set an eight-plot limit per family.

"It's hard to get into Green River," Ann Rower writes in her 2002 novel *Lee & Elaine,* which imagines the artists Lee Krasner and Elaine de Kooning as newfound lesbian lovers in death, thrown together in the afterlife in Green River Cemetery.

"Elaine wondered what it would be like to have sex with Lee. 'Now that we are—'

Lee wondered how she was going to finish the sentence. Now that we are 'alive?' 'Dead'?

'—What?'

'—friends.'"

Much of the first part of the novel is a rumination on the loss of Rower's friend, the artist Hannah Wilke, who was buried at

Green River following her death in 1993. The overarching theme of *Lee & Elaine* is about these two female artists whose work was overshadowed by their artist husbands, Jackson Pollock and Willem de Kooning, respectively. For many pages, Rower tries in vain to locate Lee Krasner at Green River. Finally, with the help of a groundskeeper, she finds her.

Krasner went on painting and working after Pollock's death in 1956. Though he was certainly up-and-coming at the time of his death, his paintings only made serious money posthumously. As the beneficiary from those sales, Krasner was able to work and to create a foundation for young artists that would eventually become the Pollock-Krasner Study Center.

She dedicated the land and creek behind the house to the state for nature preservation so that it couldn't be developed. She covered the floorboards of the small barn studio so she could go about her own painting. When she died in 1984, Pollock's splattered floorboards were perfectly preserved.

Six months after her death, the Museum of Modern Art gave a retrospective of her work. She is only one of four female artists who have received a retrospective at MoMA.

It is a bit tricky locating Lee at Green River. Pollock's stone is massive, at the top of a small hill at the back of the cemetery. There is a much smaller rock just a few feet directly in front of his, in actuality, his footstone. This is the grave of Lee Krasner.

Abstract painter Jimmy Ernst is one of the artists who did make a home in East Hampton. The son of surrealist artist Max Ernst, he secured his father's release from Nazi-occupied Paris. Unfortunately he could not get his mother, art historian Luise Straus, out. She was murdered at Auschwitz.

Jimmy moved to East Hampton in 1969 and died of a heart attack while waiting to give an interview on his newly published memoir at radio station WMCA in Manhattan in 1984. Just next to his plot, marked by a smaller vision of Pollock's boulder, is a small plaque with a quotation attributed to him that seems to argue for Green River's importance:

> *Artists and poets are the raw nerve ends of humanity*
> *By themselves they can do little to save humanity*
> *Without them there would be little worth saving*

Though Green River might be a sore spot for locals, as the resting place for some of the greatest artists of the twentieth century it has become a mythical place for those who give a damn about what's worth saving, as Jimmy Ernst put it.

As women, artists like Lee Krasner, Elaine de Kooning, and Hannah Wilke had to go to extraordinary measures to be taken seriously by the art world. De Kooning took to signing her paintings with her initials, lest she be identified as a woman, or worse, as the wife of Willem de Kooning.

Just as in a museum, to read the names of these female artists next to those of their male counterparts at Green River puts them on rightful equal footing. A young aspiring artist who makes the pilgrimage to the grave of Jackson Pollock might stumble upon that of Hannah Wilke and want to know more about her. Here's hoping.

GHOSTS OF NEW YORK

SLEEPY HOLLOW CEMETERY, TARRYTOWN

Joan Didion wrote that "we tell ourselves stories in order to live." One could argue that we tell ourselves ghost stories in order to understand.

Scary stories told at sleepaway camp or at slumber parties are amplified with dramatic effects: the flashlight under the chin, pitch darkness, a strange place. These stories are instructive: don't drive home late at night, don't pick up hitchhikers, and whatever you do, don't go in the cemetery.

A little girl hopes to prove she's not scared of the local cemetery—what could there be to be scared of? Boys dare her to stick a knife in the ground of one of the graves, proving she was there. Off she goes; she walks up to the tombstone, sticks the knife in the ground, and turns to leave. But wait. She can't move! Something is holding her back. *Someone* has got her! She dies of fright.

The poor thing had stuck the knife in her dress, pinning herself to the ground.

Cemeteries are embedded in our national consciousness as deeply terrifying places. Why do we go to such great lengths to mythologize them this way?

Sleepy Hollow Cemetery, in Sleepy Hollow, New York, is synonymous with cemeteries in most American minds thanks to "The Legend of Sleepy Hollow," by Washington Irving. I can still remember the sheer terror I felt watching Ichabod Crane walk across the Headless Horseman's Bridge in the animated Disney version, the frogs croaking his name: "Ichabod, Ichabod, Ichabod."

The Headless Horseman is a Hessian soldier, a German mercenary or "sell-sword," who fought for the British during the American Revolution. The tale goes that the horseman was decapitated by a cannonball during battle and his ghost rides every night, looking for his lost head (but willing to take another in its place), then booking it back to the cemetery where he was buried before sunrise.

Tarrytown and Sleepy Hollow are essentially the same place. The town of North Tarrytown voted to use the name Sleepy Hollow in 1996. (There is a Tarrytown, however, which still exists to the south.) For nonresidents, Irving's love for his adopted home has rechristened this place as Sleepy Hollow forever.

Washington Irving was born in New York City, the son of Scottish and Irish immigrants. Named for George Washington, he was born in 1783, the year the Revolutionary War ended. An outbreak of yellow fever sent him out of the city to the safe fresh air of the country, to Sleepy Hollow. It was here he was charmed by the locals and their ghostly legends.

In her excellent introduction to the Penguin Classics edition of *The Legend of Sleepy Hollow and Other Stories*, Irving scholar Elizabeth L. Bradley describes Irving as the "first American writer to achieve international renown," "the architect of America's founding mythology," and "a Brother Grimm for the new world." She describes the Headless Horseman as "the new nation's first ghost, appearing in the first American ghost story."

Though he would travel throughout the United States and Europe in his adult life, Irving always considered Sleepy Hollow

his home, so much so that he bought a grand estate there and named it Sunnyside. After serving as minister to Spain, Irving returned home to Sunnyside in 1846 and died there in his bedroom of a heart attack in 1859.

I have visited Irving's grave several times. My first trip was during an anniversary weekend to the restaurant and farm Blue Hill Stone Barns. We stayed the night in Sleepy Hollow and the next morning took a detour to the Old Dutch Church, where I forced my future husband to take photos of me cheesing in front of Irving's grave and the site of what was once the Headless Horseman's Bridge. His grave is easy to find, given the fact that the small path on which it rests is called Crane Lane and includes a helpful sign that says "Irving" with a portrait of the writer himself and an arrow pointing the way.

The Old Dutch Churchyard and Sleepy Hollow are two separate cemeteries. But with his famous ghost story, Washington Irving made sure that it was impossible, truly, to separate them. The fact that his eternal resting place is in the churchyard of the Old Dutch Church and not Sleepy Hollow Cemetery means that the two burial grounds are forever tied together, despite polite protests from their superintendents.

Irving has an excellent view of the entire cemetery of the Old Dutch Church, which rests down the hill near what I would imagine as the Headless Horseman's Bridge. The colonial residents of Sleepy Hollow, whose true stories inspired Irving, men and women who forged a life in this little hamlet near the river and who bravely defended themselves from British soldiers, rest here in dappled rows down the hillside.

Upon my most recent trip to Irving's grave there was a large tour group standing in front of his family plot, not really listening to the guide but snapping photos. I waited for them to pass on and made my way over.

There was the carcass of a small squirrel missing its head at the foot of Irving's plot. I warned a young boy standing near me to watch out. "Oh God," he said, noticing the rodent, "that's *awful.*" I laughed, but he was right; the sight of blood and carnage in a cemetery was sort of awful.

The Revolutionary War can feel so removed from modern consciousness that it seems bloodless. Later, in the helpful pamphlet on the history of the church, I read the story of a young mother, one of the permanent residents of the churchyard, who fled her house under attack by the British and Hessian soldiers who set it aflame. Realizing she had left her baby inside, she broke through cover, ran back toward the house, and was stopped by a soldier who had rescued the baby, placed her in a blanket, and put her safely behind a shed.

Sleepy Hollow Cemetery and the Old Dutch Church are the exception to the rule about American cemeteries. Americans, and plenty of European tourists, actually *visit* these cemeteries. Responsible parents from different parts of the United States take their cranky middle schoolers here, hoping they will learn something about American history. European guidebooks list Sleepy

Hollow as a notable American historical site, and its proximity to the city, just a short train ride out of Grand Central Terminal, makes it a popular place for tourism.

In addition to its historic import, Sleepy Hollow is still an active cemetery. Queries I had about peculiar graves within its borders went unanswered by its superintendent. "Our historic records are not open to researchers," rang the familiar refrain. The good news is, however, that the cemetery itself is open to the curious.

At about ninety acres, Sleepy Hollow is much smaller than Green-Wood or Woodlawn. It was established in 1849, when

New York City was just beginning to understand it was running out of burial space. Tarrytown, in the beautiful Hudson River Valley, home to the grand estates of the Rockefeller family, became prime eternal real estate.

Walking through Sleepy Hollow—and it is certainly walkable—is like walking through a haunted house occupied by America's most prominent industrialists and tycoons. Just near the main entrance to the cemetery is the resting place of Andrew Carnegie, the second wealthiest man of the period. He and his wife lie beneath a large but, all things considered, humble Celtic cross forged with granite mined from his family estate in Scotland.

Just outside the Carnegie plot is the tombstone of union organizer Samuel Gompers, the founder of the American Federation of Labor. The irony of these two major figures of American industry and its labor laid to rest directly across a small path at Sleepy Hollow is a fitting introduction to the cemetery.

Looking up the hillside, the Rockefeller mausoleum glistens white against the sun, like the capitol, with several other small tombstones implanted in the slope as if in supplication.

This is the mausoleum of the less flashy Rockefeller brother, William. When most people talk about a Rockefeller they mean his older brother, John. Though equally involved in the family business, Standard Oil, William was more inclined toward privacy, as his mausoleum indicates. Though the structure itself is very impressive—a Greco-Roman temple at the top of the hill with a nice view of the cemetery and almost, nearly through the tall trees, the river—his name appears only in small script at its bottom left-hand corner.

Surrounding the mausoleum are several other slab tombs in the circular lawn. One belongs to a daughter of William, Geraldine, who married Marcellus Hartley Dodge, president of the Remington Arms Company. Resting alongside Geraldine is her only child, named for his father. Marcellus had taken up flying as a hobby. Thinking it too dangerous, Geraldine sent her son to

France as a graduation present; tragically, and rather ironically, he died there in 1930 at the age of twenty-two in a fiery car crash. Geraldine went on to have a vibrant career in dog shows and became the first woman to be invited to judge the Westminster Kennel Club show. When she died in 1974 at the age of ninety-one, she was laid to rest here, next to her son.

Just beyond the Rockefeller mausoleum is another beautiful tomb, that of another oil tycoon, John Dustin Archbold. The dome shape makes the mausoleum stand out, though sadly its most stunning feature, a brilliant blue glass mosaic ceiling, can't be

seen from the outside. Though Archbold and John D. Rockefeller were competitors in business, they were friendly in their personal lives. When JDR's wife, Laura, died and he was unable to travel to Cleveland to bury her (because of his legal troubles), Archbold gladly housed her remains in his mausoleum until JDR was able to travel nearly five months later.

As I was taking photos of the Archbold mausoleum from the Rockefeller plot, a lone car drove up to the mausoleum's circular drive.

"Working on a Saturday?!" a man called, incredulous.

Why do women always laugh in situations where they feel uncomfortable?

I laughed. "Nice day for a walk."

"Does this mean you get to take Monday and Tuesday off?" the stranger asked.

I peered into his car. He had a large dog in the backseat.

"What do you mean?"

"I don't mean anything. I'm confused."

Later, when my driver picked me up after my long day in the cemetery, he asked, "Why do you think people think cemeteries are scary?"

"I suppose because death makes people uncomfortable."

"But dead people can't hurt you. Only the living can hurt you."

Beyond the Archbold mausoleum is another one of Sleepy Hollow's legends: the Bronze Lady. As I walked up the path, the Bronze Lady sat with her back to me, facing the mausoleum she guards, the resting place of Civil War general Samuel Thomas. Thomas's widow had the sculpture commissioned for his tomb but wasn't happy with the outcome, claiming she had wanted something more "gay."

The Bronze Lady is apparently haunted. According to legend, visitors hear her weeping at night and say that she cries tears of blood. If you touch her, something either something very good or very bad will befall you. One local resident claimed after a visit to the Bronze Lady that her Camaro was crushed by a falling tree limb. I'm generally content to exist somewhere between those two extremes and thus far I have refrained from touching her.

Every time I visit the Bronze Lady I come away with a different vibe. Upon my first visit she looked incredibly sad, her heavy

eyelids peering down at her gigantic feet. Then I noticed her enormous hands, her shrouded hair.

The anecdote about Archbold and John D. Rockefeller is a heartwarming one, though in reality most of these titans of American industry were corrupt or, at the very least, guilty of corrupt business practices. While the Rockefellers were also prominent philanthropists, the family's legacy is controversial. When we talk about the 1 percent today, men like Amazon founder Jeff Bezos, it's a conversation that began with the Rockefellers. At one point, JDR was worth $900 million. Today, that would be $21 billion. As of November 2019, Bezos's worth topped $108 billion.

As I walked up the path thinking about my strange interaction with the man in the car with the dog, it struck me that the Bronze Lady might not be sad. Maybe she's just really, really tired. Sick and tired.

I tried to shake off the slimy residue of white male privilege in search of one of Sleepy Hollow's prominent female permanent residents, Elizabeth Arden. But as usual, I got a little lost. On a wrong turn down a path I came across a gorgeous family plot in the hillside, the resting place of the Speyer family, with a gigantic tombstone depicting three women, one seated with a dog at her feet. The epitaph seemed to explain its meaning:

And now abideth faith hope charity these three but the greatest of these is charity

A quotation from 1 Corinthians 13:13, a note, perhaps, for the 1 percent on the other side of the hill.

Continuing on in hopes of finding Elizabeth Arden, whose real name was Florence Nightingale Graham, I came across a wooded pathway. After I struggled through cobwebs and mosquitos, a gigantic Greek Revival mausoleum appeared through the brush. I rounded the corner to see if I could locate a family name. There it was: Chrysler, the resting place of William Chrysler, the head of the automotive corporation and builder of Manhattan's Chrysler Building, once the tallest building in New York City until it was surpassed by the Empire State Building in 1931.

As mausoleum expert Doug Keister points out in his book *Stories in Stone: New York*, it's ironic that the mausoleum is in Greek Revival style rather than Art Deco, since the Chrysler Building is one of the finest examples of Art Deco architectural design in the world. Oh well!

I never did find Arden, but near the Chrysler mausoleum I was surprised by the sound of rushing water. I was near the Pocantico River at the cemetery's border. At one time the river supplied the Old Croton Aqueduct, which gave New Yorkers clean water from 1885 until 1965.

The Pocantico River is a tributary that flows into the Hudson. The Hudson River gives the entire region its lushness and wildness, and gives the city an essential resource. Here's where I make the obvious analogy of the sound of the river being a reminder of a source of life, an artery of renewal. Where most bodies of water in cemeteries are man-made, Sleepy Hollow's nature feels more genuine because it is.

A large plot stands alone just above the river, with one gigantic mausoleum atop it. Initially I went in for a closer look because I spotted unusually modern stained-glass windows that depict the New York City skyline. I walked up the path and around the front to find the name, and there it was, in huge letters: Helmsley.

New Yorkers are well-acquainted with the name Leona Helmsley, the "Queen of Mean," a woman who was unapologetic about her cutthroat business practices in New York City real estate ventures, which included fraud and tax evasion. But I wonder if Helmsley gets more attention for her bad behavior because of her gender.

Leona Helmsley is also notorious in cemetery history.

When her husband Harry died in 1997, he was entombed in the family mausoleum at Woodlawn Cemetery in the Bronx. But when the cemetery began construction on a community mausoleum too close to her family mausoleum for her taste, Leona sued Woodlawn for $150 million and moved Harry to a new mausoleum at Sleepy Hollow. This mausoleum reportedly cost $1.4 million. Leona also left $3 million for perpetual care, including the request that the mausoleum be steam cleaned at least once a year. Good news, Leona: the mausoleum was sparkling clean when I visited. It looked brand-spanking new.

The fact that Harry and Leona made their money through real estate makes the eternal real estate snafus all the more fitting.

When Leona died in 2007, she solidified her reputation as an eccentric rich person by leaving $12 million to her Maltese dog, Trouble, in her will, and instructions for him to be buried with her in the mausoleum. No word on whether these wishes were carried out, because sadly it's illegal for the remains of pets to be buried in human cemeteries in New York State.

Harry's epitaph reads, "I wait for the time we can soar together again." Leona's, for all the gossip of her being a hard-ass, says, presumably to Harry, "I never knew a day I did not love you."

The river is just a short walk down a hill from the Helmsley mausoleum. It was at least a ten-degree temperature difference in

the shade, and next to the river there was a nice, cooling breeze. On the other side, people were out walking their dogs. There were a few memorial benches scattered alongside the bank.

I was desperate for lunch and a glass of ice water. I decided to take a break, walking up Dingle Road from the cool shade of the trees by the river and back into the blinding sun. A small tour group made its way down the street, the members chatting about the heat.

Rounding the corner I caught a glimpse of white amongst what at first appeared to be an overgrown area of brush. I inched closer. Columns of a structure emerged, then a small staircase.

It was a mausoleum, hidden in the green overgrowth.

I climbed down the stairs, waving away gnats, spiderwebs, and mosquitos that were also eager for lunch. This was a unique mausoleum: small and square, but flanked by freestanding columns and with unusual modern brass lattice covering the glass door. I could barely make out the name, to the right of the entrance, so I took a photograph, afraid to venture farther into whatever creatures might await me in the sunken grass.

Later I looked carefully at the photo and zoomed in on the name.

Albert D. Lasker
1952

Lasker is considered by many to have been the father of American advertising. He acquired Sunkist as a client in 1908 when the orange business was practically bankrupt. Amongst his many firsts in the field of advertising, Lasker convinced Americans that orange juice was a health drink, saving the orange farm industry from certain annihilation.

Albert and his third wife, Mary Lasker, were prominent philanthropists, particularly in the field of medicine. They were also passionate art collectors. By the time Albert's health began to decline in 1951, they were already the proud owners of several paintings by Henri Matisse. In preparation for the inevitable, the Laskers asked Matisse, through his son Pierre, a prominent art dealer, if he would be willing to design their mausoleum at Sleepy Hollow. Mary said she wanted something "light, gay, and not at all somber."

This mausoleum, completely obscured from view, is the design of none other than Henri Matisse.

The Laskers paid $25,000 for the mausoleum. When Albert died in 1952, Mary asked Matisse if he'd be willing to create a design for a stained-glass window that would be installed at the back of the mausoleum, facing the river. Matisse was also in poor health. By this time he was working primarily in his now famous cutouts, which allowed him to lie in bed rather than stand all day at an easel. He obliged, and sent Mary the cutout for "Ivy in Flower." For whatever reason, Mary didn't like the design and rejected it, much to Henri and Pierre's disappointment. But she still had to pay for it. Henri died in 1954 and "Ivy in Flower," in its cutout form, went on loan to the Art Institute of Chicago, and later the Dallas Museum of Art.

Mary died in 1994 at the age of ninety-three and was entombed in the mausoleum at Sleepy Hollow. As the founder of a number of charities related to medical research, she said, "I am opposed to heart attacks and cancer and strokes the way I am opposed to sin." As I was researching the backstory of the Lasker mausoleum, a series of photographs made of it in 1956 turned up, housed in the Library of Congress.

If you had shown me the mausoleum I saw at Sleepy Hollow compared to these photographs, I would've swiped right by them, incredulous that they could be the same structure.

The Lasker mausoleum still stands, now a weathered brown, nearly buried by nature and the passage of time. The back window where Matisse's "Ivy in Flower" would have hung is a plain pane of dirty glass.

At the time I encountered the Lasker mausoleum, I knew nothing about it. All I had were the photographs on my phone and the mental note to go back to investigate. The Lasker mausoleum is not on the list of notable sites on Sleepy Hollow's map. It's almost completely obscured from view. The fact that I had walked by it and noticed it through the dense trees and bushes is something of a miracle. There was a moment when I thought, "What is that? Oh, forget it. I'm starving." Instead, stomach growling, I went to look.

The discovery of the Lasker mausoleum encapsulates what is so magical about cemeteries and what kind of secrets they hold, made all the more magical in a cemetery like Sleepy Hollow, which does appear in the history books. Even here, there are still stories to tell.

The path brought me back to the fork in the road near the Carnegies. I stopped in the community mausoleum, hopeful for a restroom, but all I found was a very quiet crypt with a lovely stained-glass window of the Old Dutch Church, complete with tombstones. It was a charming meta-tribute, a portrait of the cemetery inside the cemetery.

On my way down Lincoln Avenue toward the Old Dutch Church, I noticed the stones were changing; they were getting

older, but not before a few Gilded Age monuments rose impressively just off the main path. Fertilizer businessman Edwin Lister's monument features a beautiful sarcophagus tomb relief with a bust of him and the complete figure of a young woman contemplating his loss, a piece of paper grasped in her hand.

Just on the other side of the drive there was one of the most attractive monuments I saw that day, that of John Hudson Hall, paper entrepreneur and later railroad magnate. His memorial contains a large slab fronted by an impressive angel who guards the family plot of Hall and ten other members of his family.

At the top of the hill overlooking the Old Dutch Church there is a large family plot with impressive statuary, the resting place of Revolutionary War general Daniel Delavan. Jesus greets you, arms outstretched. Behind him, a young woman (or angel) bearing the cross sits atop a very tall, thin pedestal. Just across

the path is Sleepy Hollow's Revolutionary War memorial, a stout obelisk with the names of the men from Tarrytown who perished fighting for the birth of their new country.

Dazed, I had stumbled off the main path and onto a backroad at the river side of the cemetery. Aside from a few mausoleums built into the hillside, there were no stones. I wandered along the grave path, grateful for my sturdy sneakers, and emerged on the other side of Washington Irving's gravesite.

It was just after Memorial Day and many of the graves in the churchyard had American flags marking the resting place of a Revolutionary War veteran or, in some later cases, veterans of the War of 1812. When "The Legend of Sleepy Hollow" was published, the Revolutionary War had ended only thirty-seven years prior.

The narrator of "The Legend of Sleepy Hollow," Diedrich Knickerbocker, claims that one of the things that makes Sleepy Hollow special is its inability to change: "For it is in such little retired Dutch valleys, found here and there embosomed in the

great state of New York, that population, manners, and customs remain fixed, while the great torrent of migration and improvement, which is making such incessant changes in other parts of the restless country, sweeps by them unobserved."

He could, in this passage, just as easily be describing the nature of cemeteries. While massive changes go on around them, cemeteries stay the same, "like those little nooks of still water, which border a rapid stream ... undisturbed by the rush of the passing current."

I have several photographs of myself in front of Washington Irving's grave. His tombstone, white and usually marked by an American flag, sits back from the

path and his family's gate, standing out. From photo to photo I look remarkably different with the passage of time, or poor choice of hairstyle. Irving's tomb, like the rest of the cemetery, stays the same, though the changing seasons make their appearance.

Perhaps this total stasis, this lack of change, makes cemeteries too permanent and therefore terrifying to the living. To get around our discomfort with the idea, we assign cemeteries a place at the outskirts of our consciousness. When we cannot avoid them we do the best thing we can do: we give them a story. We give them ghosts.

As Knickerbocker points out, "There is no encouragement for ghosts in most of our villages, for they have scarce had time to finish their first nap, and turn themselves in their graves, before their surviving friends have travelled away from the neighbourhood, so that when they turn out of a night to talk the rounds, they have no acquaintance left to call upon."

I love the idea that ghosts don't exist—or at least don't reveal themselves to the living—because there is no one there to reveal themselves to.

Ichabod Crane is an outsider to Sleepy Hollow. He is a schoolteacher with hopes to woo the wealthiest Dutchman's eligible young daughter and to build a life for himself here. He is intelligent, but superstitious, and he has competition in Brom Bones, a former soldier and expert horseman who is also after Katrina's affections. Though in numerous film and television adaptations Ichabod prevails over the Headless Horseman, in Irving's legend Ichabod vanishes into thin air. After his encounter with the horseman, all that remains is his hat and a shattered pumpkin.

While all the old wives of Sleepy Hollow insist that Ichabod was carried away by the Hessian ghost, the more likely explanation is perhaps that he fled Sleepy Hollow out of fear and that Brom was masquerading as the horseman as means of intimidation. Or, worse, that Brom, costumed as the horseman, took the opportunity to annihilate his competition for Katrina in a more permanent manner.

Other than "The Legend of Sleepy Hollow," perhaps the story Washington Irving is best remembered for is that of Rip Van

Winkle. Nagged by his wife, the colonist wanders into the woods to hunt squirrels and meets some strange men playing nine pins. They offer him some liquor, which he drinks, and he falls into a deep sleep. When he wakes up, his musket is old and rusted and his beard reaches down to his feet. In the village, everyone asks how he voted in the last election. Perplexed, he exclaims his allegiance to King George. Running into a familiar-looking young woman, he asks her name. It turns out she is his daughter. Somehow he had slept for twenty years in the Catskill Mountains, completely missing out on the American Revolution.

Rip's magical story, waking up in a foreign land, is an elaborate metaphor for America after the Revolutionary War. The surroundings and the people were the same, but the colonies had been reborn as a new country. Despite the fact that no time had passed, for new Americans, independence meant they had awoken in a new era and a new, foreign country. Unlike the long and storied history of England, Americans had to create their own history. Irving put this theory to work in his first book, *A History of New York*, with Knickerbocker as his narrator. As Elizabeth Bradley puts it, Knickerbocker's book is "a kind of Old Testament for New York." Irving is its author, the author of the legend for a new country desperate for definition. America may be a young country, but that doesn't mean it's any less in need of a working mythology.

On my way out of the cemetery, one obelisk stopped me in my tracks when I noticed there was a small clock embedded in its granite. "My father's clock," it read, "placed here at my request."

Research turned up an article in *Americana* magazine published in 1920 on Sleepy Hollow by a writer named Caroline Williams Berry. Berry had also noticed the "curious monument" and wondered about its origins. She wrote: "The audible ticking above the mortal remains of a man seventy-one years, silent in death since 1880, made one stop to think how short, how transitory, human life is."

Reading Berry's description, I thought back to my time standing in front of the same clock wondering, like her, over its origins. Though by the time I stood there, nearly one hundred years later, it wasn't audibly ticking.

Or was it?

THE ROAD NOT TAKEN

KENSICO CEMETERY,
VALHALLA

I had not planned to write about Kensico.

I had not planned to write about the way the cemetery unfolds, in rolling hills, on the drive that cuts it into two gigantic sections.

I had not planned to write about Valhalla, New York, in Westchester County, or how the person who named the hamlet was obviously a Richard Wagner fan.

I had not planned that I would get out of the car and feel overwhelmed by the sheer expansiveness of the place, all 461 acres of it.

Kensico, I thought, I could write about in a small blurb, a mention—"other cemeteries of interest." But Kensico would not be degraded or downsized.

When I got in my ride share on the way to Kensico my driver said its name like it was a place he knew. "Have you ever been there?" I asked. He paused, then quietly said, "Yes."

I didn't ask.

When we pulled through to the entrance, chosen at random, it became obvious that Kensico represented what's tricky about cemeteries. There is so much to see that any decision you make feels like the wrong one.

"Calm down," I told myself. "I'll just look for two notables: Ayn Rand and Anne Bancroft. Whatever I come upon along the way will be a bonus. Surely, that'll give me a few hours here and that will be enough to see."

Latitude and longitude coordinates come in handy when you're in a cemetery as gigantic as Kensico and you need help locating a specific grave. Ayn Rand was easy enough to find. She was just a short walk from where my driver had dropped me off, near Mineola Lake, with its picturesque fountain and the Landon mausoleum, guarded by twin Peter Lorre–looking sphinxes.

There is something sinister about Ayn Rand. I'm not sure where I got the impression that anyone carrying a copy of *Atlas Shrugged* is a person to avoid. I have still never read her work. It's both impressive and terrifying that in 1991, in a reader's poll taken by the Library of Congress, *Atlas Shrugged* was named by readers as the most influential book they had ever read, second only to the Bible.

I think Ayn Rand, the woman who had a six-foot-tall floral arrangement in the shape of a dollar sign next to her casket at her funeral at Frank E. Campbell in Manhattan, would have loved

Kensico Cemetery. Rand believed that vision of the individual was the most powerful tool in society. There are several monuments at Kensico that illustrate the power of capitalism. In its expansiveness and beauty, Kensico transforms memorialization into some kind of power.

Rand is buried alongside her husband, a man named Frank O'Connor. O'Connor was an actor when he met Rand, and seems to have given up his career in support of hers. After her enormous success afforded them a wealthy lifestyle, he took up painting and weathered several lengthy affairs of Rand's, mostly with younger men. Rand said in interviews she never could have written anything worth reading without O'Connor's support, calling her books her "temples" to him.

I had seen Ayn Rand, so I punched in the coordinates for Anne Bancroft. According to Google maps, it looked like she was all the way at the top of the hill on Katahdin Avenue. I began my slow but steady walk up the path. At each vista I stopped to take a

few photographs. At the top of the hill the cemetery looks down at the Taconic State Parkway, and behind the mountain—to call it a hill is really an understatement—is the Hudson River and the Tappan Zee Bridge.

A statue of a grieving woman caught my eye. This turned out to be the resting place of Peter DeRose and his wife, May Singhi Breen DeRose, both jazz musicians of the Tin Pan Alley era, best known for the songs "Somebody Loves You" and "Deep Purple." Peter's memorial contains a touching letter from May, which includes a lovely epitaph: "Every friend he ever made, he kept."

There was a group of cars another level above me. I paused to give them some time, thinking it might be a funeral. But as the cars passed me on the way back down the mountain, I saw that the men inside the vehicles weren't dressed for a funeral. They were dressed up but sporting red bow ties. Once I'd reached the area they had vacated, I saw a large tablet flanked by two Greek sphinxes. This is the Mecca Temple of the Ancient Arabic Order of the Nobles of the Mystic Shrine. In front of it, there were about a dozen now empty folding chairs and a speaker's podium.

I had stumbled upon a secret meeting of the Shriners.

After what felt like a very long walk up the hill, it seemed like I had finally reached the top. But Kensico surprised me again. There was a whole other cemetery up here. The top of this mountain I had just climbed was not a peak but rather an entirely flat plot of land, the size of most average cemeteries. I must have walked for half a mile before coming to the other side of the "peak," and looking down, I could see endless sloping grass and more tomb-stones. From here, I couldn't see the end of Kensico. It stretched on, forever.

In this section there were lots of memorials typical of the late 1800s, mostly Catholic, large crosses and Christograms. I looked down at my phone. It claimed I was right on top of Anne Bancroft. I scanned the area for a monument vaguely resembling photos I'd seen of hers. Nothing. I did another quick Google search. Different coordinates turned up. Bancroft was nowhere near here. I had walked up the mountain for nothing.

But, of course, that wasn't true. Up the mountain I had seen Peter DeRose, I had seen the secret meeting of the Shriners. I had seen countless memorials and I'd gotten a great idea of how large this place is. I wiped the sweat beading off my brow and got on with it. If I followed Katahdin Avenue back down the other side of the mountain, I could eventually get to Seneca Avenue and to the Jewish section, Sharon Gardens. It made more sense for Anne Bancroft to be there. She was, after all, married to Mel Brooks.

With a renewed sense of purpose I made my way down the avenue. Every fifty yards or so there were small turnabouts with

memorials in a center island. This made walking down the avenue very difficult, because every time I came to a turnabout I had
to decide which side to walk down, the right or the left. Feeling
anxious about missing things, there were some I walked fully all
the way around, taking a peek at every monument and section
in the complete circle. Pausing briefly at one to take account, I
looked down to the right of where I was standing. There, on a
small bronze plaque read in bright green, "In memory of Frances
E.G. Coy, born 1886, lost on S.S. *Titanic*, April 15, 1912."

What if I hadn't walked to that side of the turnabout?

Who knew what I was missing. I doubled back. I wandered
into complete sections. There were treasures everywhere. A girl in

a ponytail drove by in a baby-blue Volkswagen convertible, smiling. Other than that, there was no one, just the drone of the landscapers down the hill.

Suddenly there was a very odd mausoleum a few yards from the street. It looked like a giant wasp's nest. I recognized it from a guidebook I'd read: the Mayer mausoleum. According to Douglas Keister, *the* expert on cemetery symbolism and mausoleums, it is a "tumulus, one of the oldest formal burial monuments." Kensico, in the cemetery cell-phone tour, compares it to the tomb of Jesus Christ. It looks like a gigantic boulder. But even Keister is not sure about its origins: "Little is known about Louis Mayer or the seven occupants of the Mayer tumulus-style mausoleum."

What if I hadn't doubled back?

I hadn't planned on writing about Kensico.

In the distance, under the shade of a large tree, I saw the friendly face of what looked like a dog. A statue of a dog, maybe. No, a lion. Two lions. Two sweet lions, sitting, nestled together, twins. Like sphinxes. There was a tombstone in front of them

that read "Shipley," but then there were two plaques directly under them, one for a woman named Elizabeth, "beloved wife and mother," and the other for a girl named Flora. I couldn't make out their last names. Mother and daughter? The lions seemed to be meant as protectors but they also looked soft, daring me to pet them.

I kept walking. I wondered briefly if I'd ever find Seneca Avenue and if I'd ever get out of Kensico. "Maybe I'll be here for hours," I thought. "What if my extra charge on my battery runs out? Surely there is an administrative building. What will I do, call I cab? Come on, there was a whole civilization without cell phones. But then I won't be able to take photos."

Just ahead I saw the girl with the ponytail standing at the foot of a stone. Where was her car? She jauntily walked away, and I meandered over to see what she'd been looking at.

It was a tombstone for the Conover family, nearly every square inch covered in text. "Laura Louise Scattergood," it read, "The Loyal, Loving, Unselfish, Sacrificing Wife of Richard Grover Conover is buried here. She died in Washington D.C. February 12, 1938. Beloved by all who knew her." Wow. "Richard Grover Conover. Died Nov. 30, 1940." "Dickie, Lilly, and Mac Little Babies of Richard Grover and Laura Louise Conover. Buried St. Michael's Cemetery, New York City." "Richard Scattergood Conover Son of Richard Grover and Laura Louise Conover, who died Aug. 2, 1927 in Michigan City, Indiana and is buried there." The poor Conovers. All of their children had predeceased them.

Did the girl with the ponytail know the Conovers? Or was she a stranger learning about them, same as me?

I heard her drive off, I saw the baby-blue Volkswagen. I saw her ponytail in the breeze.

Finally, I was coming to a fork in the road. That must mean I had reached Seneca. Would it have been weird to ask the girl with the car for a ride?

There was a huge obelisk at the fork in the road. I got closer. It was the Actors Fund. Another thing on my list for Kensico. Thank God.

The Actors Fund was established in 1882 mostly to support out-of-work vaudevillians, who, by the time this monument was erected in 1941, were destitute. Several members, hundreds, probably, are buried here alongside the obelisk, which is flanked by two female figures holding masks and bears the inscription "The play is done the curtain drops /slow falling to the prompters bell."

What if I had found Anne Bancroft? What if I'd gone the right way to see her and missed this?

My driver on the way to the cemetery had recommended that I try to see the Asian section. "The stones," he said, "are something else." I was sad to add another thing to my list that I just wouldn't have time to see, or even the ability to find. As I rounded Seneca Avenue, my head throbbing, I wished I had thought to bring a bottle of water with me.

Then I saw them. The dragons. I was in the Asian section. I had found it.

What if I had gone the right way?

There were several gigantic family tombstones, all in gold flake and black marble, guarded by the laughing faces of Chinese dragons on the hillside, looking down at the road I'd driven in on. "Wong," "Chan," "Cheng," some in Chinese characters, others with epitaphs in Chinese and English. "A well-loved and kind

lady," one said. "You warmed all of our hearts. You will always be dearly missed." Next to the Chinese families were Hungarian families, Polish names, Italian names. One for a professor of engineering: "an encyclopedic mind, a generous heart."

At the bottom of the hill, there was a stooped elderly man who had parked his car and was placing a bouquet of flowers at a grave. I hung back by the Chengs to give him his privacy. He walked slowly back to the car. I thought he was leaving. He returned with a bottle of water and poured the entire thing onto the flowers. Across the lawn, another middle-aged man stood loudly praying over one grave, his arms outstretched like a preacher.

I looked down at my phone. Anne Bancroft was just across the street, it said, in Sharon Gardens, which, unsurprisingly, is larger than most Jewish cemeteries. Entire synagogues own plots here. To call it a "section" is misleading. It is Sharon Gardens. It's its own.

Carefully I crossed the street. An intense cyclist barreled toward me in the ninety-degree heat. I walked into Sharon Gardens. The GPS told me Anne Bancroft was right here. I looked to my right. I looked to my left. I looked forward. I did not see her.

Luckily, I had the section number. I had a map. I even had her plot number. I would find her. I looked over, and there was a large family gathering at a gravesite. Not that way.

I doubled back. I went the other way.

I walked all the way to the back of Sharon Gardens. I couldn't understand why Anne Bancroft was so elusive.

When I was sixteen I had a literary-themed costume party for my birthday. I rented a gorgeous dress and said I was Katerina Van Tassel from Sleepy Hollow. One of my best friends dressed up as Mrs. Robinson from *The Graduate*. I always thought it was a really good costume, but isn't *The Graduate* a movie, not a book? It is a novel, actually. A novella, 1963.

I've always been drawn to Anne Bancroft. She seemed to me like a serious actress and she married a funny guy like Mel Brooks and they seemed really happy. Also, she was beautiful. She died of uterine cancer, and my grandmother died of ovarian cancer. None of Anne Bancroft's friends even knew she was sick, because she was a private person.

I kept walking. Eventually, I had to pass another family making their way back to their cars. I tried to walk behind the cars, so they wouldn't be bothered by my presence. But one of the teenage boys saw me and looked at the woman who was presumably his mother as if to say, "Who's that?" and she responded by tilting her head and shrugging. It is amazing to me how much we can communicate by not even speaking at all.

It had become incredibly hot and my headache had gotten worse. I spotted the administrative building in the distance, past Sharon Gardens, and I thought, "Maybe they are open." Sometimes, cemeteries are short-staffed on weekends. But there were lots of families in the Sharon Gardens section so I twisted the doorknob in hope and was met by a blissful blast of air-conditioning and a bustling office fully staffed with several women who helpfully asked me if I needed anything and if I was looking for anyone in particular.

I said I wanted a map and asked where the bathrooms were.

Why didn't I ask about Anne Bancroft? What if I'd gone straight to the administrative building, asked where Anne Bancroft was, found her, walked through Sharon Gardens, and then left? What if I'd decided Kensico was just too big? The mountain unscalable?

I left the bathroom. A large Asian family came into the bathroom "rest area" and were boisterous and seemed happy to be at Kensico.

What if I hadn't gone to find Ayn Rand first?

I called my car. It was the same driver from before. The Asian family seemed to have arrived in a small tour bus parked outside the rest area.

"I thought that might be you," my driver said. "Did you get everything you need? Did you see everyone you wanted to see?"

I never found Anne Bancroft.

"Yes," I answered him. "I did."

What if I hadn't doubled back?

"You know, it's funny," he said. "You asked me if I'd ever been to Kensico."

He turned up the air-conditioning.

"I have actually spent a lot of time here."

I wanted to find Anne Bancroft. I had a plan to find Anne Bancroft.

"My mom is here. My mom is buried out here."

I had not planned to write about Kensico.

SACRED AND PROFANE

FERNCLIFF CEMETERY, HARTSDALE

You haven't experienced true silence until you've walked through an empty mausoleum.

My first thought walking through the halls of Ferncliff Mausoleum is usually something along the lines of "Who knew that my shoes were this noisy?" Every step I take is a constant reminder of the persistent beat of my heart, my status as a living, breathing person amongst the storied dead. Ferncliff tries to dampen the click-clack of my shoes with Oriental carpets underfoot. But the thunderous sound of footsteps still echoes rooms away, making it all the more disarming when I hear absolutely nothing.

It would be incredibly expensive, not to mention totally unnecessary, to heat this enormous mausoleum, so, in the colder months, teeth chattering, I thank my lucky stars I didn't leave my coat in the car, pulling it tighter around me. Walking through Ferncliff Mausoleum is like walking through a cathedral, marble eyes staring down at you. But in a cathedral the dulcet tones of the choir echo throughout the nave. There are the sounds of people quietly praying, or struggling to the pews.

This is real silence.

There is something different about a mausoleum. Ferncliff designed it this way. Ferncliff is a cemetery, by definition: its business is burying people. And there are in-ground burials there. But the real spirit of Ferncliff is its mausoleums, of which there are three. These are not the small, private, family mausoleums that you will find in larger cemeteries like Green-Wood and Woodlawn. These are gigantic, community mausoleums with several floors. Here, these floors are cut out of marble and enshrined with stained glass.

The main mausoleum, sometimes called the Cathedral of Memories, was completed in 1929, designed under the supervision of James Baird, who collaborated on the Lincoln Memorial and the Tomb of the Unknown Soldier. Its marble halls contain four floors of entombed crypts, more than fourteen thousand crypts and counting, fifteen thousand niches for cremains, and three hundred family rooms (private corners that contain room for six to eight entombments). Like a prefab house, a family crypt at Ferncliff can be enhanced with any number of additions, the most notable of which is a custom-made, Tiffany-style stained-glass window.

Practically every corner of the main mausoleum contains treasures. One visit, I noticed a small plaque at the foot of a crypt that made it stand out from the other numerous tombs that filled an entire hallway. As it turns out, it is the resting place of Alice Lovejoy, a Women Airforce Service Pilot (WASP) who died in an airplane crash in service of her country on September 13, 1944.

Directly across the hall, a small niche for cremains bore several bright pink lipstick kisses. Its epitaph read "Adorada Madre," adored mother.

Visitors are rare to Ferncliff's oldest mausoleum. As I walked down the hallways, entire floors were nearly completely dark. The lack of light added to the eerie silence and made the fantastic stained-glass windows all the more impressive as the mausoleum's only light sources.

One marble column I passed bore the epitaph "Precious Blossom." Parents addressed their daughter: "God loaned you to us for twenty glorious years. Sing on, darling." I shared the information for this memorial online, and a friend came back with the story: the young woman had died in a car crash on a treacherous patch of interstate.

The immense structure, which represents both the presence and the loss of these people, is a different experience from a cemetery where mostly everyone is in the ground. Here, the dead are built up, memorialized in expensive materials like stained glass and marble.

Most guidebooks to Ferncliff focus on its celebrity population and their dates of arrival: Malcolm X, in 1965; Judy Garland, in 1969 (since moved to Los Angeles's Hollywood Forever); Ed Sullivan, in 1974; Joan Crawford, in 1977; Thelonious Monk, in 1982; James Baldwin, in 1987; pop star Aaliyah, in 2001; and China's Madame Chiang Kai-shek, in 2003. Like many cemeteries in New York before 1980, Ferncliff had a Madison Avenue office, where wealthy New Yorkers could come to peruse catalogs and purchase their plots or family rooms at Ferncliff on a pre-need basis.

The Madison Avenue office probably accounts for some of the celebrity burials, as does the fact that high-profile funeral homes, like Frank E. Campbell, also located on Madison Avenue, frequently recommend clients. But with those exceptions in mind, Kevin M. Boyd, the president of Ferncliff Cemetery, describes Ferncliff as a neighborhood cemetery. "The East River might as well be the Atlantic Ocean," he laughs.

Ferncliff is a family business. Kevin's father was president of Ferncliff Cemetery, taking over for a man named Cornelius F. Bastable, or CFB. (Initials often function as cemetery nicknames due to signatures on correspondence and internal documents.) CFB and Boyd's father, Vincent J. Boyd (VJB) met because they attended the same Catholic parish, St. Andrew Avellino, in Flushing, Queens.

VJB was a tax attorney by trade and eventually became the general counsel for the cemetery. When CFB retired, he took over as Ferncliff's president until he had to go down to Columbia Presbyterian for open-heart surgery in 1993. Kevin, by that time, was well-acquainted with the family business. He started working summers at Ferncliff when he was nineteen. There was a union foreman whose workers used to give him a hard time about having to manage the boss's son, so he would be purposefully tough on Kevin, just to let his guys know what was what.

"Back in those days, the cemetery was run like a mom-and-pop business," Boyd says. "The level of personal trust—you hired people you knew, people you could trust." But a family-style approach to business didn't dampen Ferncliff's sales. Most of its business came through walk-in traffic. In the main mausoleum there's still the wood-paneled waiting space for the bereaved or for potential pre-needs, which looks like something out of the production design for *Mad Men*.

Kevin seemed tickled by my passion for Ferncliff. "Why Ferncliff?" he asked.

When you truly love something, explaining why is sometimes difficult to put into words. The reasoning is complex. To me, Ferncliff is like a tiered jewelry box. Every layer reveals something precious.

Ferncliff is not like the other cemeteries in this book. Driving past it, on Secor Road in Hartsdale, you might think it a golf course. There are no raised tombstones to indicate it is, in fact, a cemetery, and the three mausoleums are well set back from the road. They could be office buildings.

Up a winding, rather steep drive from the first mausoleum are Ferncliff's other two community mausoleums. Unlike Ferncliff Mausoleum, you won't find silence in its second mausoleum, the Shrine of Memories, completed in 1956. There is a stream of Muzak pumped through ceiling speakers. An instrumental version of Bette Midler's "From a Distance" played while I tried to capture the right lighting for photographs of the stained-glass windows.

Near the front entrance there is a couch bookended by tables with utilitarian lamps. The concrete blocks that make up the wall behind it reminded me of my middle school. As I breezed past, the

couch sagged, forlorn, as if it knew there was no hope of anyone ever sitting there.

A courtyard in the middle of the building features panels by an artist named Francesco Bevilacqua, "a painter-sculptor who has developed a technique that presents figure compositions chiseled on polished black Belgian marble through a combination of incised lines and stipple reminiscent of mezzotint," a plaque explains.

The panels depict Moses, Abraham Lincoln, Jesus, Neil Armstrong, and Galileo. "It is the opinion of the directors of Ferncliff that the selected subjects of the ancient and modern world represent individuals whose contribution to humanity will be remembered until the end of time," the panel continues. "We trust they will be a source of meditation for our visitors."

There are flowers, more flowers than in Ferncliff Mausoleum. It seems that the Shrine of Memories was active until the 1980s, presumably leaving the dearly departed there with more surviving visitors today. Attached to one bouquet of flowers left at the foot of the wall crypt was an announcement of a daughter's confirmation.

I thought I was alone in the Shrine of Memories, until an older lady disembarked from a rickety elevator, her two adult children following reluctantly behind her. "Hey," she said to a friendly but tired-looking security guard, "can you look somebody up for me?"

Between the Muzak and the kitschy panels, the Shrine of Memories is pretty charming. If Ferncliff Mausoleum is the responsible, straight-laced older sibling, the Shrine of Memories is its hippy, ne'er-do-well sister. The presentation of figures like Moses and Abraham Lincoln seems to indicate that there is some kind of greatness about being entombed in Ferncliff. This sort of Judeo-Christian salesmanship is very common in memorial park cemeteries, and it reminds me of one of my all-time favorite cemeteries, Forest Lawn, in Los Angeles, California, the most influential of all modern American cemeteries.

Shortly after World War I, a man named Hubert Eaton had the idea to make cemeteries more appealing—to make them look less like cemeteries—in hopes of drawing customers into the cemeteries to buy plots in advance. The idea that a person would plan their family plot in advance was almost unheard of at the time. This sort of "pre-planning," as it is known today, was reserved for the extremely wealthy. Eaton theorized that if you could make cemeteries less "ghastly," then people would be more excited about visiting and, in turn, purchasing space for eternity.

He called these cemeteries "memorial parks," and his influence is felt all over the United States. The modern cemetery that most Americans are familiar with is a memorial park, with flat plaques in the ground rather than standing tombstones. Memorial parks from the street look more like parks, or golf courses, than they do cemeteries.

In many ways, Ferncliff is the East Coast's answer to Forest Lawn. Eaton and his followers needed a way to make the cemetery appealing—to make their cemetery *the* cemetery that everyone would want to spend eternity in. They got around the "no cemetery

cemetery" look of the memorial park through the creation of the grand mausoleum.

An early advertisement for the cemetery in *Fortune* magazine features Ferncliff's mausoleum prominently: "Its advantages over dismal ground burial are obvious. Within immaculate marble crypts, the departed are safely laid to rest, forever secure, forever protected against the elements."

It might seem ironic to modern Americans, who have embraced cremation as their preferred method of burial, to "protect" our dead from the "elements." But Ferncliff's three mausoleums are indicative of the "memorial impulse," as Eaton described it, which typified American society after World War I and well into the baby boomer era of the 1950s and 1960s. Eaton is the cemetery's first entrepreneur. As described by David Charles Sloane in his excellent book on the history of cemeteries, *The Last Great Necessity*, the Forest Lawn way "commercialized the burial ground."

By the time Ferncliff was founded, New Yorkers had little need for the park cemetery. They had actual parks for recreation and for much-needed green space in the city. As Manhattan was rapidly expanding at the turn of the century, people fled the city for the security and safety of the suburbs, a cyclical practice that has continued as in-demand, gentrified neighborhoods run out of space and rents reach astronomical proportions. It's no coincidence that Ferncliff, with the first mausoleum of its kind in New York City, was planned and built in the suburbs, in a hamlet called Hartsdale.

In fact, it's for the same reason—lack of space—that mausoleums exist. A large mausoleum of this kind functions as a sort of apartment for the dead, making the most of space. The mausoleum's benefit to a cemetery is, for the most part, to maximize the number of crypts for sale. As Ferncliff's director in 1977 told the *New York Times*, "We have four floors here and, with six bodies per floor, we get twenty-four in the ground space of one."

During my last visit to Ferncliff I was struck by an inscription in one family's crypt, from a poem by Longfellow: "This life of mortal breath is but a suburb of the life elysian, whose portal we call death." Life on earth as only a transition to the eternal life of the great beyond is a traditional Judeo-Christian concept. But in this case the word "suburb" seems particularly apt.

The suburban home, with more space, removed from the dangers of city life, is one that Americans used to plan on. Young couples saved for their first home with the idea that it would be a respite from their professional lives. New York City planner Robert Moses made the commuting lifestyle not only a reality but a dream for many New Yorkers, whose jobs remained in the city but who wanted a more peaceful home life in the suburbs.

New York is one of the most expensive places to live. It is also, unsurprisingly, one of the most expensive places to be dead. As of 2002, it cost $4,500 to be buried in the ground at Ferncliff and $15,500 for one space in the mausoleum. Two spaces in the mausoleum can cost upward of $22,000. Cushy additions, like stained-glass windows, are undoubtedly extra.

The rise of the memorial park cemetery in America is directly related to the rise of the suburban, white, upper-middle-class. Eaton's memorial park, like suburbia, hopes to marry the benefits of country life with all the perks and conveniences of city living. Memorial parks are the cemetery version of the suburbs.

But some notable burials at Ferncliff, like Malcolm X, Thelonious Monk, and James Baldwin, are ground burials. There are no maps or signage to their graves. Latitude and longitude coordinates are the best bet for locating them. My first trip to Ferncliff I spent close to twenty minutes (even with the correct coordinates) trying to locate Malcolm X on an extremely cold November morning, my boots sinking into the mud.

One of the problems of the memorial park as the suburban version of the cemetery is that it brought with it all the inclusionary and exclusionary practices of suburban living. "Memorial parks presumed instead that lot-holders wished to be buried with those neighbors with whom they had some cultural or religious affinity," Sloane writes in *The Last Great Necessity*. As Kevin Boyd said, despite its celebrity interments, Ferncliff has always been a "neighborhood" cemetery.

Like Forest Lawn and nearly every single cemetery in the United States, for decades most memorial parks carried a racial clause in the fine print. Cemeteries excluded people of color from the basic human right to burial.

Forest Lawn's racial clause stated, "No interment of any body or the ashes of any body other than that of a human body of the

Caucasian race shall be permitted." One particularly heinous episode is the case of Sergeant Rice, an eleven-year veteran of the US Army who had been killed in the Korean War in 1951 and was barred from burial at his neighborhood cemetery, Sioux City's Memorial Park, in Iowa City, because he was Sioux. Unbelievably, the funeral and graveside service had already been completed when cemetery officials walked up to the grave and prevented Sergeant Rice's coffin from being lowered into the earth.

When President Truman learned of this, he was disgusted and arranged for Sergeant Rice to be buried at Arlington. But these racist clauses in cemetery policies continued across the country well into the 1970s.

It is a tragic but unsurprising fact in American history that racism extends as far as the grave. Standing over the resting place of civil rights leader Malcolm X (or Hajj-Malik El Shabazz, as he was known after his conversion to Islam) and writer James Baldwin, who are both buried at Ferncliff, I often think of Baldwin's words on patriotism: "I love America more than any other country in this world, and, exactly for this reason, I insist on the right to criticize her perpetually."

Thousands of people come to pay their respects to Malcolm X at Ferncliff every year. And there is another more modern celebrity at Ferncliff who draws crowds. The pilgrimage to her grave represents the enormous inspirational influence of popular music when combined with tragic early death. Aaliyah was only twenty-two when she was killed in a plane crash in 2001. She is entombed in a back corner crypt in Ferncliff's newest mausoleum, the Rosewood Mausoleum. Her father joined her there in 2012. Her epitaph reads simply, "Baby girl."

By the 1990s, the Shrine of Memories was nearly at capacity, and Ferncliff was desperately in need of another mausoleum. Cemeteries are, after all, a business. And to make money you have to have space. The living residents of Hartsdale weren't enthused about the idea, claiming that a large mausoleum would affect their views. (Views of what is not clear.) Whatever the reasoning, the city of Hartsdale fought the expansion, and for six years the cemetery was embroiled in a legal battle. In the end Ferncliff prevailed, and its third mausoleum, the Rosewood Mausoleum, was completed in 1999. Its construction reportedly cost $25 million.

On my last visit, Aaliyah would have just celebrated her fortieth birthday, and Valentine's Day had just passed. Her crypt was covered in red and pink flowers and birthday greetings from fans. One letter read, "Time passes and you are still an inspiration for me and my girls. Your energy, positive light and music help me get through difficult times. I try to live by your legacy—we can achieve our dreams and still maintain being a beautiful person. You are a positive, motivating force within my life. I hope you are proud."

Rosewood is the only mausoleum at Ferncliff with space remaining. Its impressive suspended glass and marble staircase is its prettiest feature. But the most striking difference between Rosewood and Ferncliff's other two mausoleums is its smell. The fragrance of the many wilting bouquets left by mourners at the foot of two floors of crypts is enough to knock you off your feet.

Individual family rooms include a gate at the door, allowing visitors to look through but not enter. One on the second floor was

decorated lavishly: filled with tchotchkes and family photographs for a beloved grandma.

I always give funerals a wide berth when I'm visiting cemeteries. I waited patiently for one to finish at Rosewood, not realizing there is a back entrance I could've gone through. By the time most of the mourners had cleared out and the equipment for loading the casket into the wall crypt was stored away, there were only a few people left wandering around.

"Hey," the bereaved said to a friend, "it's always great to see you."

"Sure," his friend said, patting him firmly on the back. "Just wish it were under better circumstances." They both laughed. A funeral director kept watch from a small office.

For those interested in this kind of entombment, it's still a possibility at Ferncliff thanks to the Rosewood Mausoleum. Asian families in particular are finding their niche in mausoleums and cemeteries like Ferncliff, sites that offer these kind of luxury options. "It's like going to heaven," Sammy Kwan, a funeral director in Flushing, Queens, told the *New York Times* about Ferncliff in 2001. "But not everyone can afford it." According to the same article, a private family room with a "crystal chandelier, stained-glass window and bronze gates" at Ferncliff would have set you back $280,000 that year.

Chinese families are more concerned with their burial traditions than the expense. Rituals like the burning of fake money, the offering of food to the dead, choosing locations with good feng shui, and importing materials from China—these considerations are often disallowed at urban cemeteries. "According to Chinese beliefs," the *Times* reported, "a good burial spot is a symbol of eternal fortune for a family." Ferncliff, known in the business as "the Tiffany of cemeteries," is sure to lock down a good fortune.

The reality, though, is that most Americans choose what they have come to see as the easiest and least expensive option for burial: cremation. As Sloane writes in *The Last Great Necessity*, the mausoleums at Ferncliff are "period pieces." With rising costs for materials, limited space, and a dramatic decrease in the death rate by the 1950s, American attitudes toward death changed enormously. Americans' need for burial and memorialization greatly decreased as the option of cremation presented itself.

Ferncliff rose to the challenge in terms of this dramatic change in American funeral practices. Today, Ferncliff does the most cremations in New York State: about 3,330 a year, a whopping 10

percent of all cremations. Diane Arbus, Jim Henson, and John Lennon were all cremated at Ferncliff.

Like any other kind of business, cemeteries have to adapt to new trends and technology in order to survive. Cremation, for years, has by far been the most popular option for most Americans. It's understandable, but it always strikes me, especially in a place as unique and beautiful as Ferncliff, that if everyone chose cremation Ferncliff wouldn't exist. Ferncliff's mausoleums contain plenty of niches from cremains, but it's been estimated that more than half of all cremations don't make it to a cemetery. Most survivors take the ashes with them. There are no private rooms, no marble tombs, no curious epitaphs, no stained-glass memorial windows, not even a simple stone or plaque.

Ferncliff would like to build another mausoleum. Rosewood is filling up and running out of space. But the community isn't having it. The town of Hartsdale doesn't want another mausoleum. Rosewood was a battle that Ferncliff won, but it took six years. Kevin Boyd says he understands. He gets it. Which is a funny thing to say about your own business. But Ferncliff's legal troubles are reflective of the plight of the American cemetery. People want to pretend that death isn't inevitable, that death doesn't exist. They want cemeteries to be invisible.

There's that old superstition of holding your breath while you drive by a cemetery. My brother and I used to do this all the time when we were little, along with "punch buggy, 1-2-3" on long car rides. I suppose the idea is that if you hold your breath death can't get you. I get it, too. Who wants to be reminded that ultimately death comes for us all? The presence of the cemetery in our community used to serve a practical purpose. Thanks to cremation we may not need cemeteries anymore. But they have always served a philosophical purpose as well, an instructive reminder. Have we done away with that, too?

Ferncliff might look like a golf course from Secor Road. But inside its mausoleums the landscape is incredibly bracing. Up the main stairway just inside the entrance of Ferncliff Mausoleum is my absolute favorite stained-glass window. I've photographed this window at every time of year, from every angle I could think of, and yet, I had never thought to get closer than ten feet away. It's a rendering of a cross, bright pink, yellow, purple, aquamarine— the colors reflect brilliantly on the stark white marble of the cold

tombs. I asked Boyd about the window, but he wasn't sure about its providence.

Last visit, I got up close and personal. An inscription at the bottom of the window reads, "In Memory of Our Daughter Dainuvita Audrins." I had never noticed it before, but the window also contains a small city scene with towers along the sea bearing what looks like the crescent from the Turkish flag. Just below the window, sure enough, there is the Audrins family niche. Inside are the urns of presumably Dainuvita's parents, Alma and Janis, and a third urn without a name, a dainty silver crucifix draped over the top.

All of a sudden I felt woozy. I walked carefully back down the stairway, the lavender light from the window over my right shoulder, gripping the marble banister. I needed a break. I walked out of the gigantic bronze doors. The blinding sunlight and blast of hot summer air didn't do much to make me feel better.

I sat down on the sidewalk bench to steady myself and looked up at the bright blue sky, the mausoleum's sentinels set against the corners of the building. Somehow, for the first time, I noticed that my favorite window is directly above the doors to the mausoleum. From the outside looking in, it was bleak: black, gray, zapped of color. I had never noticed it before—but it was prime real estate.

A group of teenagers approached from their car, sheepish and giggling. "Excuse me, ma'am," one asked, "do you know where we could find Aaliyah?" I directed them to Rosewood. They set off, jostling each other. One girl shook her head, laughing, "I can't believe we're in a *cemetery*," and the group happily sighed, nodding with relief at her acknowledgment of their strange adventure.

Though they were well up the road, I laughed with them, realizing why I'd felt faint. Inside that incredible mausoleum, I'd been holding my breath.

YOU MADE US A FAMILY

HARTSDALE PET CEMETERY,
HARTSDALE

On a trip to the pet store to buy some food for my brother's frogs, my mom noticed an adorable reddish-brown puppy with short legs and big ears in a pen by the cash register. "Jessie," she said to me in a phone call, "there's a dog here at the pet store. I'm coming home to get you so you can come see her." That puppy became our sweet dog for nearly fifteen years. We named her Lucy.

Lucy was there through it all: my graduation from high school, every Christmas morning, any major family event. Anyone who passed through our front door became Lucy's friend. When I came home from college I would soak up time with her and then sob while giving her one last scratch and nuzzle before heading to the airport. Years passed. "There's not much we can do for her," the vet said. Lucy came home and died in her own bed. My mom buried her in our backyard.

Animal lovers know the inadequacy of the word "pet." Our pets are more than our animals. They are our friends, our companions, our family. They understand us when no one else does. In New York City, where people are more likely to put off having a family until later in life, or forgo children altogether, pets play an important role in people's lives. For many New Yorkers, their pets are their family.

It's unsurprising, then, that the oldest and largest pet cemetery in the world is located just outside of New York City. A short drive from Ferncliff Cemetery is Hartsdale Pet Cemetery, established in 1896. Situated on a long, sloping hillside, this touching little cemetery contains over eighty thousand burials. Dainty tombstones jut out of the grass, tugging at your heartstrings.

Hartsdale was founded by an equestrienne named Emily Berthet who was looking for a "dignified" place of rest for pets outside the city. She partnered with Dr. Samuel Johnston, a prominent veterinarian who had opened the first hospital dedicated to animals in New York. Legend has it that one of his clients was so distressed over the death of her dog in 1896 that Johnston offered to bury the pet in his apple orchard.

At the time, pets could not be buried in city limits. Rumors spread about Johnston's little cemetery, and with more and more requests for burials, he decided to put up three acres of his orchard. He instituted a transportation system similar to Woodlawn Cemetery's: pets at his Twenty-Fifth Street clinic in Manhattan were sent via train to the cemetery and their owners could hire a funeral carriage to follow. Hartsdale Pet Cemetery was born.

Though the vast majority of burials are dogs, there are also cats, horses, birds, primates, and, according to *The Peaceable Kingdom*, a short book on the history of the cemetery, a lion cub by the name of Goldfleck, who belonged to the Hungarian princess Elizabeth Lwoff-Parlaghy and lived with her at the Plaza Hotel.

In 2013, Hartsdale Pet Cemetery was listed on the National Register of Historic Places, the only animal burial ground to be honored this way. And, after years of petition, the cemetery became the first in New York State that allows for the interment of human cremains in a cemetery designated for pets.

Philip Seldon
Jan. 10, 1941–Sept. 7, 2016
Together Forever
With His Beloved Cats

At the top of the hill a sculpture of a German shepherd stands astride a large stone with an accompanying plaque and pole bearing the American flag. He looks off into the distance, alert and ready to rumble. This memorial is "dedicated to the memory of the War Dog, erected by public contribution by dog lovers, to man's most faithful friend, for the valiant services rendered in the World War 1914–1918."

Just to the right of the War Dog Memorial is a memorial with a Georgia O'Keefe-esque skull "to the animals we do not mourn, the millions of animals whose lives are taken for research and testing," placed here by the American Fund for Alternatives to Animal Research.

Though the monuments are impressive, what makes Hartsdale Pet Cemetery extraordinary is the personal memorials of its permanent residents. The names of all these beloved pets alone are enough to send your sentimentality meter through the roof, and

the accompanying tributes are visceral testaments to appreciation and true loss.

Dopey
11.21.89–2.5.01
Gone from Our Lives
But Never from
Our Hearts
Lambrides

Zanzi
We are so proud of you
January 24, 1969–December 18, 1978

Heidi
Steppin' Legs
You gave us so much in so short a time
Sept 5, 1971–Dec 4, 1975

Cali
You made us a family
1996–2008

Brit [and] Bobby
1924–31 1931–35
A gift from God
Dear Faithful Pals

My Heart is Broken since you went
away even my tears couldn't make you stay
Gone but not forgotten
Nov 15, 1949 Flash Nov 2, 1961
Mar 15, 1951 Dutchess Aug 27, 1967
Mr. Mrs. Consiglio

Samantha
"There Could Never Be Another to Take Your Place"
We Will Always Love You
Tom, Keith, Carmen and Ann

Seigfreid
Feb 14, 1938
Sept 6, 1949
Black Eyes. A Coat the Color of Sunshine. Gentle. Kind.
Humorous.
Beloved of Dr. & Mrs. Irvin C. Bronstein and Amber

Schweppsie Weber
4/5/61–3/15/69
Our Little Black Rose

Teddy & Tottie
They gave nothing but
Love and Affection
Julia W. Howard

Snoopy 1999–2014
You fought to stay with me but I had to release you from the
pain
I love you
Papa

Gsa Gsa
Love of my life
Until We Meet Again

When I first started thinking about writing *Silent Cities*, I knew I had to include Hartsdale Pet Cemetery. People are more comfortable being curious about a pet cemetery than a human one. On my Instagram account, photographs I've posted from Hartsdale are some of my most popular posts.

The reason behind the curiosity and popularity of the pet cemetery is that it's one rather large step removed from our fear of death and dying. When the loved one is an animal, and not a person, it makes it easier for people to engage with and express their grief. It's also a more common experience—pets have shorter life spans. If you've had pets early in life, than you've also lost pets. Frankly, our relationships with animals are also less complicated by dysfunction and more representative of our hope for unconditional love.

All it takes is one walk through Hartsdale Pet Cemetery to come into contact with real loss. Just like the pet names and nicknames we give to our furry companions, their memorials are incredibly unique. I don't have enough fingers and toes to count how many different nicknames I have for my dog, Ralph. There's a real intimacy about the memorials in pet cemeteries that I sometimes wish extended into those for humans.

It's rare in this moment in our relationship with death to see ornate or intimate memorials in our cemeteries. Perhaps there's a false sense that an intimate display of grief violates a sense of decorum. With the rise of cremation, the need for memorialization, in the form of a tombstone with an epitaph or even a small plaque, is less and less.

So many people don't know how to engage with a friend or family member who is grieving. They worry over bringing up the loss for fear of upsetting the survivor, and the bereaved might feel pressure to avoid the topic, afraid being a downer. But if your friend lost a pet, would you hesitate in the same way to check in with him or her?

The loss of a member of our animal family allows just enough space to where people feel freer to communicate their grief. It's understandable but also frustrating that we can't quite get there in our society when it comes to human loss.

On my last trip to Hartsdale there was a middle-aged woman crouched at the foot of a small tombstone near the entry to the cemetery. She had brought one of those gardening pads to kneel on, and she was hard at work clearing the grave of her late pets, pulling up weeds and picking up flowers and other knickknacks that needed to be discarded.

I gave her plenty of space, walking up to the War Dog Memorial and around the back of the cemetery, hoping that by the time I made my way back to the entrance she'd be on her way so that I could get over to that corner and explore without invading her privacy.

But when I rounded down the little hill, she was still there, wiping away at the stone with a damp towel. She paused briefly to wipe away her tears, then placed her arms around the top of the stone in a mournful embrace.

WE REMEMBER

CEMETERIES OF MANHATTAN

Behind a gigantic mosaic made up of blue tiles, you will find this quotation from Virgil, the words forged in mangled steel: "No Day Shall Erase You From the Memory of Time."

The blue tiles are not tiles at all, but 2,983 individual watercolor drawings. As a complete piece they are entitled *Trying to Remember the Color of the Sky That September Morning*. Each drawing is a slightly different color blue, and each represents a person who was killed on 9/11 or in the 1993 World Trade Center bombing.

The mosaic wall is a memorial, but it also serves as a divider. A small plaque explains what lies behind it: "Reposed behind this wall are the remains of many who perished at the World Trade Center site on September 11, 2001. This repository is maintained by the Office of the Chief Medical Examiner of the City of New York."

The 9/11 Memorial and Museum is both memorial and museum, as its name indicates.

It is also a graveyard. Those at Ground Zero join the thousands of people who are buried in Manhattan.

Who are these people, and how do we remember them?

Trinity Church, in Lower Manhattan, is a good place to start. Thousands of tourists come to see the church and the churchyard. Today, even more people visit thanks to the popularity of the musical *Hamilton*. Alexander Hamilton, one of our nation's founding fathers, is buried here, in Trinity Churchyard, next to his wife, Eliza. When I visited his grave last summer, waiting for others to snap their photos, it seemed that visitors—mostly young women—were more interested in Eliza than Alexander himself.

The church was under a complete "rejuvenation project," scheduled to be completed in 2020, meaning, sadly, that I could not go inside. But Trinity Church has three locations in Manhattan: the one on Wall Street; St. Paul's, just a few blocks away; and Trinity Cemetery and Mausoleum in Harlem, at Broadway and 153rd Street. Trinity uptown announces itself as "Manhattan's only active mausoleum," as if passersby might be enticed by such a sales pitch. Unlike Trinity downtown and St. Paul's, Trinity uptown bears the important distinction of being a historic cemetery but an active one, at that.

My journey to Trinity uptown had me questioning many decisions I'd made that day. By 10:00 a.m. it was nearly one hundred degrees. I'd sat on a Manhattan-bound L train for nearly thirty-five minutes, only to be greeted by another fifteen-minute delay for an uptown A train. Even with the trains running well, the commute from my apartment to Harlem is an hour and a half. That day it took me nearly two and a half hours to reach Trinity,

by which time the limits of my patience and my bladder had surely been put to the test.

I reached the hard-to-find office near the Riverside Drive entrance of the cemetery, praying to God, Yahweh, and any other deities I could think of that the building would have a bathroom. It did. Upon exiting I asked the woman sitting at the desk if I could have a map. She obliged and asked if there was someone in particular I was looking for, pointing out a route that would take me to those pertinent sites.

"We do have a funeral coming in," she said protectively.

I replied that I would make myself scarce.

"No, you don't have to do that, it's just . . . well, you know we are an active cemetery."

I promised I would be on my way, and wiping sweat from my brow, I left the glorious air-conditioning. She followed me out the door.

"Wait—" she said. "Are you . . . are you interested in cemeteries, or . . . ?"

I explained that I was writing a book about cemeteries, New York cemeteries specifically. In that case, she led me back inside, showed me a few interesting books in their collection, and gave me her card in case I had any questions.

"But," she warned. "They are very . . ."

"Protective?" I offered.

"Guarded," she said. "We are still active, after all."

I explained that I completely understood and was on my way out the door again when she offered me some candy.

"Take some of these. They are protein." I thanked her and set out again.

"I hope you are wearing sunscreen!" she called out after me.

Because usually there aren't other people to talk to—not a living soul—cemeteries can be wonderful or frustrating places, depending on your mood. In most active cemeteries, the hope of a map or a bathroom is quickly extinguished. Attendants at historic cemeteries, though, like Green-Wood, Woodlawn, and others, are more than happy to answer questions, point out sites of interest, and offer tours of the grounds.

While it's understandable that in an active cemetery (to be fair, both Green-Wood and Woodlawn are both active cemeteries, but they are just much, much larger than Trinity uptown) the cemetery staff would be a bit wary of someone like me, an overheated woman desperate for a restroom, it's also frustrating to be met with an attitude of suspicion. Cemeteries are meant for visiting and exploring. But decades upon decades of isolation and stigmatization have left them feeling . . . guarded.

Trinity uptown is cut in half by Broadway, leaving one lower section, where you'll find the more modern mausoleum, the resting place of writer Ralph Ellison and *Law & Order* actor Jerry Orbach, and the aforementioned office. There are in-ground interments all up the side of the hill, with a nest of mausoleums at the top and more tombstones behind them. Within this section are several plots of the Astors—a family that dominated New York Society for nearly a hundred years.

John Jacob Astor (1763–1848) was a German-born real estate mogul who became America's first multimillionaire. His wealth flowed through the family tree well into the 1900s, including to John Jacob ("Jack") Astor IV, who went down with the *Titanic* in 1912. His pregnant wife was able to board a lifeboat and survived. Jack's body was recovered from the sinking site, identified by his gold pocket watch, and he is laid to rest at Trinity, in one of the family mausoleums.

Just on the other side of the path there is a rather decrepit, almost sinister-looking mausoleum marked "Jumel." Rightly so—it is the resting place of the notorious Eliza Jumel, a wealthy woman who married Aaron Burr when she was fifty-eight years old. Rumors swirled that she had married him for status, and he for her money. Reportedly the union did not last long and the two separated not four months after they were married.

The Morris-Jumel mansion, the home where Eliza had lived with her first husband, Stephen Jumel, is the oldest house in the borough and, according to some, haunted. As the house is now a museum, it is frequented by large school groups. Legend has it that one rowdy group of kids was shushed by an elderly woman who looked down upon them from the balcony as they waited for their tour guide. When the guide arrived, unlocking the large padlocked door, she explained to the children that the house was empty. The woman they'd seen on the balcony, who matched a description of Eliza Jumel, had died in 1865.

By 1842, Trinity downtown and St. Paul's were at capacity, so the church created this cemetery uptown as a means of expansion.

The land is the former estate of John James Audubon, the world-famous ornithologist and author of *Birds of America*. Audubon came to the United States from his home of what is now Haiti in 1803 and swiftly contracted yellow fever. Thanks to the help of some Quaker women who ran a boardinghouse in the city, he survived. After traveling extensively in the United States and in England, he eventually purchased this New York land in 1841. Parts of the Audubon estate were sectioned off for residential buildings and the cemetery by his widow throughout the 1860s.

Audubon is buried in the other section of Trinity Cemetery, behind the Church of the Intercession on the other side of Broadway. The entrance to the cemetery puts you right in front of the

large cross that marks his grave, erected in 1893 by the Academy of Sciences, which is covered in beautiful carvings of birds and other flora and fauna.

As I walked through this part of Trinity, I noticed a residential building at the far right corner of the cemetery, covered in a mural depicting several different kinds of birds and the likeness of Audubon. Also in this corner of the cemetery is the resting place of Mayor Ed Koch. Koch reserved a plot for himself at Trinity in 2008, it being the only active cemetery in Manhattan. He died in 2013, and his epitaph, marked by both the Star of David and the New York City seal, speaks dedication to his faith and to the city he loved:

Edward I. Koch
December 12, 1924– February 1, 2013
Mayor of the City of New York 1978–1989
"My father is Jewish, my mother is Jewish, I am Jewish."
(Daniel Pearl, 2002, just before he was beheaded
by a Muslim terrorist)
Hear O Israel, the Lord our God, the Lord Is One
He was fiercely proud of his Jewish faith. He fiercely defended
the City of New York, and he fiercely loved its people. Above
all, he loved his country, the United States of America, in
whose armed forces he served in World War II.

Koch told journalists that the last words of Daniel Pearl were "as important as the most holy of all statements in the Jewish ritual." The price Koch paid for his plot has been a subject of speculation, with some reporting it might have been as high as $20,000. When questioned about the expense, Koch explained it was important that his final resting place be in Manhattan. "The idea of leaving Manhattan permanently irritates me. This is my home," he told the Associated Press. "The thought of having to go to New Jersey was so distressing to me."

As I rounded the path to the back of the church, I rumi-
nated on Koch's bold choice, both in terms of location (spare no
expense) and epitaph. Daniel Pearl was after 9/11? It's strange
how traumatic events get jumbled in your mind. Yes, Daniel Pearl
was murdered in 2002. I looked back toward the rest of the cemetery, and for a moment it looked like the ground was moving. This
was it. Heatstroke. I prepared to pass out. Thankfully, I wasn't hal-
lucinating. There was a whole flock of birds—pigeons—pecking
around the grass. There must have been hundreds of them. When
I stepped closer, they suddenly took off, flying away in a uniform
pack, just past Audubon's cross.

Trinity's third location is just a few blocks north from the
downtown location and is known as the Chapel of St. Paul's. It is
the oldest surviving colonial church in Manhattan. People sometimes get confused when I mention the fact that Trinity has three
cemeteries in Manhattan. There's downtown—"Alexander Hamilton," I usually say—then uptown, in Harlem, and then there's St.

Paul's. People usually pause here. "The 9/11 church," I say. "The one at Ground Zero." That usually does it.

St. Paul's churchyard is a meditative space amidst the hustle and bustle of Wall Street. There are several large trees that, according to believers, were spared by some divine miracle on 9/11. Their shade provides a nice place to sit and take a break amongst distinguished permanent New Yorkers.

Even though I worked in an office quite near St. Paul's in the financial district for over a year, I never traveled to Ground Zero. When the city began the long and arduous process of clearing the site and planning a memorial, I paid attention, albeit distractedly. There is no good day to visit the 9/11 Memorial and Museum. Tourists with limited time in the city will make time to visit. But as a New Yorker, when is a good time to visit? There is no good time.

But after thirteen years, I was leaving New York.

I am not a native New Yorker. I was, as E. B. White would say, one of the lucky ones. According to White, in his landmark 1949 essay, "Here Is New York," there are three kinds of New Yorkers. The first is the native New Yorker. The second is the commuter. And the third is the settler, "the person who was born somewhere else and came to New York in quest of something."

"Commuters give the city its tidal restlessness; natives give it its solidity and continuity; but the settlers give it passion."

I was a settler. For thirteen years, I felt like the luckiest person on Earth. And even after thirteen years, even though to many I had become a "real" New Yorker, I still, in many ways, felt like a settler. I still reveled in the strange, perfect energy that is New York.

So, knowing that I would soon be leaving, I looked over to my left, to Ground Zero.

I could see the ribs of the Calatrava station peeking out from behind another building, not three hundred feet from where I was sitting. I walked, hesitantly, out of St. Paul's and down the path toward Ground Zero and the 9/11 Memorial and Museum.

Alongside the Calatrava station there was a farmer's market and several concrete blockades barring vehicles from getting any closer to the memorial plaza. Several read, "Remember Love. Yoko Ono 2019."

I walked into the memorial plaza and looked up. The new tower gleamed, blindly reflective from the sun. I looked down. Then I saw the first fountain where the North Tower once stood.

The sheer magnitude of its absence, the empty space, is hard to wrap your head around. I never got a chance to go to the top of the Twin Towers. On a trip I made as a teenager with my family,

I prioritized the Empire State Building. It seemed classier, more old New York. By the time I moved to the city in 2006, the towers were gone.

For some reason the day I approached the North Tower fountain the water was off. Maybe there were repairs being done. It was eerily quiet. The sounds of tourists and visitors chatting, even laughing, made me feel ill. The water at the bottom of the fountain stood immobile like a stagnant pond.

I took a few photos and wandered over to the South Tower fountain. This fountain was on. The sound of rushing water is an essential part of this memorial. It drowned out the ambient sounds of the surrounding environment and created a sort of a peaceful atmosphere.

Then I noticed the flowers. There were a few white roses sticking out of a few of the memorial panels that line each fountain. Engraved on these panels are the names of the people who died in the 9/11 attacks. A nearby plaque informed me that on a victim's birthday, the museum memorializes this person by attaching a rose to his or her name.

The plaza wasn't crowded, but it wasn't empty, either. The vast majority of visitors appeared to be European tourists, speaking either German or French. Police stood nearby, chatting idly by the entrance to the museum, holding enormous guns. I smiled at a K-9 unit.

I stopped by one section on the South Tower panel and noticed it was demarcated specifically for United 93, with the names of the passengers.

A small boy toddled toward me, assuming my legs were his mom's. He clung to my right side, pulling on my dress. We looked at each other, perplexed. His mother ran over. "I'm so sorry," she said, laughing. They walked away, holding hands. He looked back at me; I waved, saying goodbye. He waved back.

I looked up at the new tower and wondered how anyone could work there. There are several businesses there, including all of

Condé Nast. I have friends who go to work there every day. They look out of their windows (on the south side of the building, at least) and look down into these enormous, gaping holes.

I knew I had to go to the museum, but I couldn't do it that day. I had to head to the subway, so I thought I'd go through the Calatrava station, since I'd never been inside before.

Inside this structure, you're Pinocchio in the belly of the whale, if the whale were dead and just a skeleton. Enormous white ribbing encompasses you, with streaming white sunlight covering

what is, essentially, an enormous shopping mall with the subway station underneath it.

I walked toward signs for the 4 train. A young boy and his father, who looked like they had just finished a round of golf, walked in front of me.

"Well, son"—the father was in the middle of explaining something—"there were several terrorists on each plane and they overwhelmed the pilots and took control of the plane."

They must have been in the museum or at the memorial and the boy had asked how 9/11 had occurred. I thought about the dad's use of the word "overwhelmed" and thought it a good choice.

"That's horrible," the boy said quietly.

"Oh, here's an Apple store," his mother said, joining them with another, younger boy. "Did you guys want to go in and look at the watches?" They went in.

I had the thought that maybe I should look for some new sneakers. Business as usual in New York. Commerce goes on. Capitalism smacks its lips, even as you attempt to grapple with those two enormous holes in the ground. Even as you walk through a subway station that was destroyed during the most devastating act of terrorism ever committed in the modern era, in a station that looks like a skeleton, you think, "Maybe I should get some sneakers."

I returned to Ground Zero two days later, for the early entry into the museum. The museum offers early entry (for an extra admission fee) for those who might need extra assistance getting into the museum, or who just want to have some time alone before the museum officially opens at 9:00 a.m. and the first tour begins at 9:30.

The first people in line were a Midwestern family. The father wore a T-shirt that proclaimed his status as a firefighter with his engine number on it. Three women in front of me were talking about their teenage children. "I told him," one said to her friends, "I am not raising my grandchildren."

Waiting for the doors to open, I thought about 9/11. I had been in my first or second class of the day in eleventh grade. My English teacher was in the middle of explaining something when my history teacher walked in and took her aside, to the back of the classroom, whispering something in her ear. This sort of thing was not so unusual but still seemed odd. We all looked at each other, concerned she was having some sort of family emergency. But she returned to the front of the classroom, saying nothing about the interruption. It was when I left to go to my next class that we realized something had happened.

"A plane crashed into the World Trade Tower," one girl said.

Everyone, myself included, thought it must have been a small plane, some error, like a Cessna, an inexperienced pilot, a medical emergency. Something like that.

Then the second plane hit. Then we got the news about the Pentagon. I saw my friend, whose father (I knew) worked at the Pentagon, being whisked down the hallway, escorted by several school officials. Her face was red. She was sobbing.

It was my school's decision that day not to let us watch television and to keep us in session. It wasn't until later, probably around 4:00 p.m., that I returned home and turned on the television.

It wasn't until then that I saw the footage of the planes flying into the towers, and the towers coming down—images played, in horrifying refrain, for the next weeks and months.

I think I saw those planes when I closed my eyes.

We went through security upon entry to the museum. Everyone appeared to be waiting for the 9:30 tour. I walked down the stairs, down into the entrance, completely alone. It was eerily silent. There was a woman standing at the foot of the stairs with a therapy dog, whispering to a museum employee.

I walked into the museum. The first thing I saw was a series of screens playing the sound of all the news reports from that morning. I reached a balcony overlooking an enormous cave. The slurry wall, constructed in 1966, still stands. It looks like the side of a gigantic ship, like the side of the *Titanic*.

The single column that survived after the towers fell and that functioned as a makeshift memorial stands, lonely, in the center of the cavernous space, surrounded by benches.

I was at the bottom of the sea.

The slurry wall looks like the *Titanic* but it's not the *Titanic*, joyful on its departure. It's the *Titanic*, somehow whole and enormous, at the bottom of the sea, in the enormous crypt that is the sea.

It's almost as if another dimension, another world in which 9/11 never occurred, could be resting on the other side of that enormous wall.

As I wandered along a sloping path to the bottom of the museum, artifacts and informational plaques called for attention. There is the stairwell that allowed so many to escape, to walk through the subway station and out to sunlight and to the rest of their lives, protected by glass.

It looks like something from Hiroshima, crumbling, covered in ash.

I walked down another stairwell running right next to the preserved one. That's when I saw those blue tiles. I swung around to the safe-seeming, plainly named "historical exhibit." But before I could enter, the top of the of radio tower stopped me in my tracks. It looked like the severed artery of a giant. Nearby, the elevator motor. The melted, smashed firetruck, Ladder 66. All in quick succession, standing there parked as if they had been there for centuries at the bottom of the sea.

When I was in the eighth grade we made a class trip to Washington, DC. We went to the Holocaust Museum.

One room I walked into contained only shoes. Thousands of shoes.

The next room, smaller, contained only human hair.

"Historical exhibit."

Such a benign name for something so horrific.

The Holocaust Museum in DC acted as an example, instructive to the 9/11 Memorial and Museum. How do we remember these people? How do we memorialize this horrific event?

A cemetery is a tragic place. But a cemetery in the place where the tragedy occurred adds another level of difficulty. Memorialization becomes complicated.

The 9/11 Memorial and Museum navigates these treacherous waters as well as it can. But a visitor's journey through this museum is no less torturous.

The "historical exhibit" is housed in a separate structure from the rest of the museum. You enter through revolving doors into a time line of events that day. Mayor Giuliani's schedule, the public school schedule, both suspended in alternate reality: a time line, a day, a future that never occurred.

The most disturbing images and audio recordings are in separate, small rooms off the main floor of the exhibit with disclaimers about their contents. Audio recordings of the voicemails left for loved ones from the victims in the towers or on the highjacked planes are accessible through little black listening devices that seem to dare you to pick them up and put them to your ear.

One room, which features photography of the jumpers, contains a quotation from a spectator who said that these people were making this decision, they were jumping to their deaths, and that she couldn't look away—not then—because she felt that she owed it to them to watch.

This quotation encompasses what it feels like to walk through this museum. One feels like it's the least you can do.

I looked around in desperation only to find a box of tissues at waist level, perfectly timed. By the time I entered the United 93 room, with its audio recordings of a stewardess telling her boyfriend, "I wish I could see your face again, babe," I was audibly sobbing.

An older man who had also been crying said to me in solidarity, "I don't know how anyone can sit through that without crying."

At the end of the exhibit there is a gigantic piece of condensed material from the towers. It was determined that the material melted into this meteor of destruction encompasses five floors of one of the towers, but that there are no human remains present within.

It seems impossible, to me, that anyone could be confident of that.

How do you end an exhibit like this? The museum opted to present a history of the World Trade Center before 9/11. It's nothing short of surreal walking into a history in which 9/11 hadn't yet happened.

The final room chronicles the rise of Islamic terrorism and the hunt for Osama bin Laden. One screen plays footage of two of the hijackers going through airport security in Boston. I wanted to jump through the screen and tackle them. To watch them stroll through security in an endless loop after reliving that horrible day is devastating.

On the other side of the museum, past the blue tiles, is the memorial room. In it, there is a photograph (when available) and name of every single victim of 9/11 and the 1993 bombing. A room in the center preserves the underground footprint of the south tower, and victims' names are read, with short bios, projected on a dark screen. When I passed through, a young man was described as a passionate bodybuilder who loved cooking with friends. He was thirty at his death.

There are personal mementos on loan from the victims' families, encased in glass like the artifacts of the Egyptian pharaohs. One entry included a woman's knitting. She was in the middle of completing a scarf for her grandson at the time of the attacks.

By the time I left the memorial room, the museum was packed. Tours were ongoing. There was another exhibit, *Dogs of 9/11*, but I kept walking. I went to the bathroom and splashed cold water on my face. My eyes were red and swollen from crying.

An elevator took me upstairs, back into daylight. A gift shop contained thousands of keychains, T-shirts, and baby onesies emblazoned with "FDNY" or "I ♥ NY."

Lawrence Wright's *The Looming Tower: Al-Qaeda and the Road to 9/11*, and *Let's Roll*, 9/11 widow Lisa Beamer's memoir, sat on the bookshelves, helplessly staring back at me. Outside, a young woman considered two melted steel columns while her male companion checked his phone.

In the days after the 9/11 attacks, 2,753 people were reported missing. In June 2019, number 1,643 was identified. Though his

name was not released, the medical examiner's office told reporters he was identified through DNA recovered in 2013. The bodies of 1,110 victims have still not been accounted for.

They remain here, in this space.

Anthropologists and historians tell us that the way in which we bury our dead and memorialize our dead can speak volumes about a community and culture. But the burial of our dead is also what makes us human. Humans are the only animals who bury our dead. Burial, and with it memorialization, gives us our humanity. And it gives the dead, at the very least, the acknowledgment "I was here."

However a museum at this location and a new tower might feel, the memorial fountains and the museum are, in a sense, acting as cemetery gates, as a place of burial for those still lost to us. They are marking Ground Zero as a place of enormous tragedy and as a place of memory.

Not all victims receive the same kind of protection.

Just a ten-minute walk up the street from Ground Zero there is a federal office building at 290 Broadway. Named for Ted Weiss, a Democratic senator from New York, it is thirty-four stories high and was completed in 1995. It houses federal offices for the Internal Revenue Service, Environmental Protection Agency, and Government Accountability Office.

It is also the resting place of thousands of slaves. As many as fifteen thousand people.

Construction on the office building began in 1991. While workers were digging out its foundation, they discovered "intact burials"—skeletons still in their coffins. Four hundred and sixty-one human remains were sent to Howard University for research. Investigation revealed that the construction of this building had disturbed the "Negroes Burial Ground," or, as the enslaved people called it, the African Burial Ground.

After enslaved Africans had stopped using the burial ground, it became, like much of Lower Manhattan, a landfill. Later, buildings and buildings were built, torn down, and built up again over the remains of these people who had essentially been the builders of the colony. Their forced labor had built the very city that now grew above them.

The federal government, having invested several hundred million dollars in this office building, intended on going forward with its construction. It was met with protests and outcry from the black community. Mayor Dinkins, New York City's first and only black mayor, sided with the community and negotiated for a compromise that would allow this burial ground to be protected as a historical landmark and sacred place.

Ultimately the building was completed. But its first floor had to be used as museum to tell the story of the African Burial Ground. A memorial sculpture was created and installed behind the building. The 461 people who had been disinterred for research were returned to the site six years later. Traditional African caskets were made for their bones, and black New Yorkers and Africans came from all over to celebrate their reburial, this time with traditional African rites and burial objects like flowers, shells, and jewelry.

A female park ranger greeted me after I'd gone through security. "Do you have time for a twenty-minute informational video?" I did. I was the only person in the museum. "I'll put it on for you," she said, nodding.

Visiting the African Burial Ground is a very different experience from visiting Alexander Hamilton at Trinity, or the 9/11 Memorial and Museum. This museum, which encompasses not even an entire floor of an office building but rather two small rooms, tells the incredible story of the people who are buried here. And it tells it to mostly empty rooms.

The video is told through the viewpoint of a young slave girl whose father has died of a fever. As she travels through Lower Manhattan, the story of the enslaved in New York is told in brief, along with burial traditions and the story of the site's discovery.

Mayor Dinkins, in his hearings on the site's discovery, said, "This is our Ellis Island."

In the adjacent exhibit, the characters in the video stand as mannequins, gathered around the coffin of the deceased. They are surrounded by a display on the history of the place, including a large map of the burial ground and a photographic mosaic of all the uncovered burials.

Male, thirties.

Female, infant.

They lie in their coffins.

At the back of the museum there is a panel on the conditions of the slave boats. An example of the shackles used was bolted to the wall. They were so small. I looked at my own wrists, my own ankles, and shuddered.

One illustration showed the overcrowding on a boat, thousands of desperate faces pushed together in fear. Another showed slave traders throwing the old, infirm, sick, pregnant, and young overboard to drown.

We see these same images, of human bondage, drowning, desperation, in the news today. Of absolute evil.

They lie in their coffins.

Most New Yorkers I mention the African Burial Ground to have no idea that there are thousands of slaves still buried in Lower Manhattan. The memorial sculpture outside the building was designed by Rodney Leon and is called *The Ancestral Libation Chamber*. It contains a pathway like an open shell, leading to a rushing fountain. When I was there, it was under renovation and the entire structure was covered in scaffolding and tarp, concealing it from view. The sculpture bears this inscription:

For all those who were lost
For all those who were stolen
For all those who were left behind
For all those who were not forgotten

The phrase most associated with 9/11 is a short one: "Never Forget."

I have seen this phrase tattooed on the limbs of men riding the subway, some with their engine number. Ask anyone who worked with first responders on 9/11 and he or she will know someone who died. Most lost dozens of their coworkers, their friends, their family. One day on the subway I noticed a man with one tower on

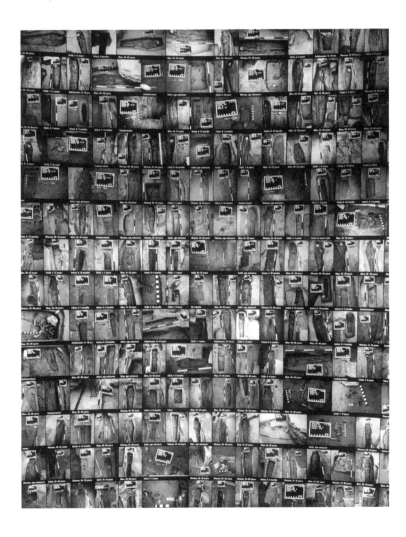

each calf muscle, both smoking and engulfed in flames, the words "Never Forget" over each.

"Never Forget" is borrowed from Holocaust remembrance. Since 9/11, Holocaust Remembrance Day uses an inverse of the same sentiment: "We Remember."

Places like the 9/11 Memorial and Museum are controversial. A friend whose brother was a firefighter that day told me his brother was enraged that they would build anything at Ground Zero. A museum was enough. But another office building? Disgusting. He vowed to never return there.

"It's a cemetery," he said.

Cemeteries occupy a strange, uncomfortable liminal space in our national consciousness. Though they began as a necessity, it's debatable whether that remains true. But then, should cemeteries that are also places of enormous tragedy or historical import go unmarked? And if you mark them, how do you do so?

The island of Manhattan complicates this issue even further. Manhattan doesn't have the space to fully commemorate the dead. By the late 1840s, Manhattan had essentially run out of space for cemeteries and therefore supported the Rural Cemetery Act in 1847 that would allow for cemeteries to be planned outside city limits. Calvary Cemetery, now one of the largest cemeteries in the United States, was founded the following year.

New York is a city that picks up the pieces and regenerates at lightning speed. It does this so frequently that one can hardly remember what stood there before. But, as E. B. White writes, "it carries on its lapel the unexpungeable odor of the long past."

And though the city barred burials not long after the Rural Cemetery Act was passed, there was little it could do about the past.

The oldest Jewish cemetery in North America is in Manhattan.

It is the first cemetery of Shearith Israel, the oldest Jewish congregation in America. This congregation was initiated by twenty-two Jews who fled persecution during the Inquisition in Brazil and thought they'd try their luck in New Amsterdam. In

1654, they landed in New York. Their first cemetery contains several graves of Revolutionary War soldiers and the resting place of the first American-born rabbi.

The remains of the cemetery are in Chinatown, behind a building at the corner of St. James Place and Oliver Street. The cemetery is usually closed to the public, though officials do open the gates once a year at Memorial Day to lay flags for veterans. Otherwise the cemetery is barred and gated, with a gigantic padlock.

St. James Square is covered in trash. A colorful mural attempts to bring some cheer. When I was there, a homeless man, shirtless and covered in tattoos, lay sprawled, passed out on the ground in front of the cemetery, his shopping cart of all his possessions nearby amongst a carpet of broken glass and garbage.

The second cemetery of Shearith Israel is tucked away in a small triangle behind a building on the corner of Eleventh Street and Sixth Avenue. Founded in 1805, it is marked by a plaque. The tombstones rest against the brick wall of what probably used to be

an alley. There is one short obelisk and one standing crypt. Like the first cemetery it is barred and gated. Visitors leave stones, in Jewish tradition, resting on the gates.

The third and last cemetery of Shearith Israel, established in 1829, is just around the corner from Trader Joe's on Sixth Avenue and Twenty-First Street. Its entrance is flanked by a Citi Bike station. The cemetery is wedged like a courtyard between three giant condominiums. It is also gated and locked.

The morning I'd set out for these three cemeteries, it was gorgeous outside—about seventy-two degrees, and there was a nice breeze. By the time I'd left the third cemetery, it was sweltering

hot. People went about their business, walking to get an iced coffee, or rushing across the street, late to work. A large truck unloaded supplies at the back of Trader Joe's. People, including at one point, several police officers, eyed me suspiciously as I snapped photos of the cemeteries, sticking my phone in between the gates to get a good view.

The receptionist at Trinity Cemetery reminded me politely that it is an active cemetery. She meant "active" in the sense that they still bury people there. They still have funerals. But all cemeteries are "active." They still "act" as cemeteries despite the fact that they have no new burials. People remain there.

All of Manhattan is, in a sense, a graveyard. Underneath all the buildings, the commerce, the progress, the development, and the buzzing life of the greatest city in the world are all the former iterations of New York that came before.

"To a New Yorker," E. B. White writes, "the city is both changeless and changing." And the power Manhattan holds over its settlers has much to do with its ability to change and still maintain a sense of being that makes it stand apart from other cities. "New York is peculiarly constructed to absorb almost anything that comes along . . . without inflicting the event on its inhabitants; so that every event is, in a sense, optional, and the inhabitant

is in the happy position of being able to choose his spectacle and so conserve his soul."

In this section White is writing about acts of violence—for example, that someone can get shot down the street in New York City and a New Yorker will walk by, unbothered. It is perhaps the same attitude that helps us to forget that upwards of fifteen thousand slaves are buried in Lower Manhattan, or that the oldest Jewish cemetery in North America is nestled in a dirty alley in

Chinatown, or that the 1,110 people still missing from 9/11 are still at Ground Zero.

The cemeteries of Manhattan may not be active burial places. But they are, still, very much active places of memory. What is the reverberating phrase from all these places of mass tragedy? Never Forget. We Remember.

It's hard to believe that anyone could forget 9/11 and its horrors. And yet, the horrors of slavery, of mass genocide, committed here in the United States often go unacknowledged in our national discourse. The African Burial Ground was covered up again, this time by a federal office building. There are millions of people now living who did not witness 9/11. Though it might seem distasteful to us, having the people who did not witness 9/11 walk through the museum is a promise we make to future generations that we will remember.

And the dead remember, even when we do not.

"The subtlest change in New York is something people don't speak much about but that is in everyone's mind," White writes, in closing. "The city, for the first time, is destructible. A single flight of planes no bigger than a wedge of geese can quickly end this island fantasy, burn the towers, crumble the bridges, turn the underground passages into lethal chambers, cremate millions."

White wrote this in 1949.

And, horrifyingly, it happened.

Ground Zero, and those lost to us there, are forever embedded in the city. And the city is our memory. But the city also goes on—it is actively changing.

On my way back to the subway after visiting the 9/11 Memorial and Museum, I was stopped by two men carrying commemorative booklets about 9/11.

"Look at this," one said, gesturing to a photo of the tree at St. Paul's that had survived.

"I know," I said, noticing he was wearing a tag that said he accepted all major credit cards. "It's amazing that the tree and the church survived."

"Where you from?" he asked.

"I'm from here," I answered.

"Oh," he said, smiling, withdrawing his sales pitch, "a New Yorker."

ACKNOWLEDGMENTS

As a new mom, I found writing this book a daily battle, and it could not have been done without the support and encouragement of my husband, Graham Roberts. Many thanks and much love to my family: Mom, Rob, and Nick, Howard and Helen, for all your love and support, and for putting up with me the many times I said, "Anybody interested in grabbing a couple of burgers and hitting the cemetery?"

Thank you to Lisa Alpert at Green-Wood Cemetery, Susan Olsen at Woodlawn Cemetery, and Ferncliff president Kevin Boyd for your openness and generosity. Thank you to Columbia University Avery Library archivist Shelley Heyreh for her assistance with the Woodlawn archive.

Many thanks to Cailey Hall for being an excellent editor, reader, and friend. Childcare assistance from Bethany Saul, Kelsey Kinderkneckt, Caroline Grogan, and the wonderful teachers at ABC Child Center made it possible for me to work. Thank you to Paragraph Brooklyn, a fantastic writer's space. To my friends and family who supported me and the Kickstarter campaign for the Silent Cities pilot, and to all our followers on Instagram, thank you. Your support is everything.

Thank you to my agent, Katelyn Detweiler, for believing in my work and this book, to my editor Amy Lyons for bringing it into the world and my excellent production editor Kristen Mellitt for making it the best it could be. Thank you to my son, Roman. I love you. I love the way you say, "Oh, wow! Look at this!"

FURTHER READING

The American Way of Death, Jessica Mitford

Famous and Curious Cemeteries, John F. Marion

Inventing the American Way of Death, 1830–1920, James J. Farrell

The Last Great Necessity, David Charles Sloane

The Legend of Sleepy Hollow and Other Stories, Washington Irving, ed.
    Elizabeth L. Bradley

"Mr. Hunter's Grave," collected in *Up in the Old Hotel*, Joseph Mitchell

Stories in Stone: New York: A Field Guide, Douglas Keister

Sylvan Cemetery: Architecture, Art and Landscape at Woodlawn, Charles
    D. Warren, Andrew Scott Dolkart, et al.

This Republic of Suffering, Drew Gilpin Faust

INDEX

Niblo mausoleum, 23
Niblo, William, 23
O'Connor, Frank, 142
O'Hara, Frank, 98
Old Dutch Churchyard, 115
Oliver, King, 55
Olmsted, Frederick Law, 8
Orbach, Jerry, 195
Parsons, Alfred Ross, 23
Piccirilli brothers, the, 60, 63
Piccirilli, Attilio, 60
Pierrepont, Henry Evelyn, 7, 14,
Pollock, Jackson, 98, 107, 109
Pollock-Krasner House and Study
    Center, 98
Rand, Ayn, 140, 141, 142
Rattner, Abraham, 98
Reed, Jonathan, 68, 70, 73
Reed, Mary, 71
Reinhart, Ad, 71
Roach, Max, 54
Robinson, Bill "Bojangles," 71
Rockefeller mausoleum, 118, 119
Rockefeller, William, 118
Rogers, James Gamble, 46, 59
Rosewood mausoleum, 167, 169
Rural Cemetery Act, 70, 76,
    86, 215
Sharon Gardens, 144, 150, 152
Shrine of Memories, the, 160,
    161, 167
silver cord, 71

Sleepy Hollow Cemetery, 112,
    115, 116
Stafford, Jean, 98, 100
Steel, Courtney, 101
Steel, Robert, 101
Stein, Jean, 102
Steinway mausoleum, 23
Steinway, Henry, 10
Steinway Jr., Henry E., 23
Straus, Isidor, 58
Sullivan, Ed, 158
Thomas, Samuel, 120
Tiffany stained glass, 44, 50, 157
Triangle Shirtwaist Factory fire
    memorial, 70
Trinity Cemetery and
    Mausoleum, 192, 197
Trinity Churchyard, 192
Van Ness Parsons mausoleum,
    22, 23
Van Winkle, Rip, 135
Vanderbilt, William, 34
Vaux, Calvert, 8
War Dog Memorial, 179, 189
West, Nathanael, 84
Wiggins, Thomas "Blind Tom," 71
Wilke, Hannah, 98, 106, 108, 109
Williams, Cootie, 55
Woodlawn Cemetery, 34, 36,
    63, 125
Woolworth mausoleum, 39, 40, 45
Woolworth, Frank Winfield, 38

ABOUT THE AUTHOR

Jessica Ferri started her career in publishing at FSG. Since 2009, she's been a freelance writer and her work has been published by the *New Yorker's Page Turner* blog, the *Economist*, NPR, Yahoo!, *Bustle*, *Time Out New York*, the *Lineup*, the *Barnes and Noble Review*, and the Daily Beast, where she is a regular contributor on books.

Jessica has always harbored a passion for the macabre, whether it be horror movies, cemeteries, true crime, haunted histories, or Charles Addams, and the list goes on. She launched *Silent Cities* (@silent_._cities) as a travelogue through Instagram, where she chronicled the incredible cemeteries she'd visit along with their unique and largely forgotten stories. The project immediately garnered the interest of a niche but very dedicated community of people who are fascinated by cemeteries and the secrets they hold.